D0449089

ANOTHER
SUCH VICTORY

by Thomas E. Baker

*The story of the American defeat
at Guilford Courthouse that helped win
the War for Independence*

Library of Congress Cataloging in Publication Data

Baker, Thomas E
    Another such victory.

    Bibliography: p.
    1. Guilford Court House, Battle of, 1781. I. Title.
E241.G9B34   973.3'37   80-28936
ISBN: 0-915992-06-x   AACRI

Copyright ©1981 Eastern National, 1997 printing
Designed by Winston Potter

Picture credits: Chapter openings and cover illustration by Don Troiani, courtesy National Park Service. Troop movement plans prepared by Division of Central Map Service, United States Department of the Interior, August 1971. All other illustrations from the Picture Collection of the New York Public Library.

Eastern National provides quality educational products and services to America's national parks and other public trusts.

Manufactured in the United States of America.

Preface

Well before dawn on a cold, late winter morning in 1781, Lord Charles Cornwallis's 2,000 British soldiers rose from their comfortless camp at Deep River Friends Meeting House, and, without pausing for breakfast, began a 12-mile march to the hamlet called Guilford Courthouse.

With the possible exception of days when the court of pleas and quarter sessions convened in the building that lent the small community its name, Guilford Courthouse was a tranquil North Carolina piedmont community. However, the rural county seat was astir with unaccustomed activity on March 15, 1781. The previous night, the 4,400 men of Maj. Gen. Nathanael Greene's American army had bivouacked around Guilford Courthouse. For nearly two months these rebels and Cornwallis's redcoats had marched and countermarched, circling each other like a mismatched pair of boxers, Greene maneuvering constantly to avoid an exchange of blows with the British, Cornwallis pressing doggedly to strike down his adversary. At long last, Greene was willing to risk an engagement, and Lord Cornwallis hastened forward to oblige him.

By nightfall, the name Guilford Courthouse would signify a good deal more than a remote seat of government in the forests of central North Carolina. For here, in one of the most bitterly contested battles of the American Revolution, Lord Cornwallis's redcoats met and defeated Nathanael Greene's rebel host. But the cost of this victory was exorbitantly high. At day's end, 500 of the finest British troops in North America lay dead or wounded in the fields and thickets surrounding Guilford Courthouse. Crippled by the loss of one quarter of his army, Cornwallis abandoned both the pursuit of Greene and his plans for the conquest of North Carolina. Instead, he chose to withdraw from the state, marching his decimated army into Virginia, where, seven months later, his redcoats were trapped at Yorktown and forced to surrender to superior French and American forces. Because the losses suffered on March 15, 1781, were an important element in the complex equation that led Cornwallis to make this ill-fated decision, the British triumph at the Battle of Guilford Courthouse was, in reality, a harbinger of final American victory in the War for Independence.

"Another such victory would ruin the British Army."

—Charles James Fox addressing the
House of Commons when news of the Battle
of Guilford Courthouse reached London.

The War in the South

THE CHAIN OF EVENTS that led two great armies to meet at Guilford Courthouse was initially forged in London in late 1777, when the government of King George III was forced to make some difficult decisions regarding the conduct of the war in America.

Since the outbreak of hostilities at Lexington, Massachusetts, in the spring of 1775, British military activity in America had been largely confined to the northern colonies. Although the British armies had at first enjoyed considerable success, neither side was able to win a decisive advantage. The war in the North seemed stalemated until the autumn of 1777, when events took a decided turn against the British.

A plan to isolate New England from the southern colonies backfired and instead resulted in the surrender of Gen. John Burgoyne's army at Saratoga, New York. This defeat emboldened Britain's ancient rival, France, still smarting over the loss of her North American colonies in the Seven Years' War, to form an alliance with the infant United States.

King George's ministers were keenly aware that this development would radically alter the strategic picture of the conflict. Although the war in the northern colonies was deadlocked, the addition of French land and naval forces might well break that logjam. Furthermore, French entry into the conflict meant that the war would likely spread from the North American continent to Europe and beyond, thereby straining still further Britain's already insufficient pool of manpower for her armed forces. Therefore, Sir Henry Clinton, British commander-in-chief in America, was issued secret instructions for the campaign of 1778. He was ordered, in part, to cease virtually all offensive operations in the North and, instead, to direct his efforts toward the South.

The British had carried out no major operations in the South since 1776. In that year, an attempt to raise the loyalist Scotch Highlanders of eastern North Carolina was smashed at the Battle of Moore's Creek Bridge, and an attack on Charleston, South Carolina, was repulsed with heavy British losses.

Despite these early failures, the British believed a major effort in the South could be successful in 1778. The South was much less densely populated than the North, and it would therefore be difficult for the rebels to raise large forces to oppose the king's troops. In addition, as long as the main British army remained around its base in New York City, it was unlikely that American Gen. George Washington would risk detaching large numbers of troops from his own army to aid in the defense of the South. Furthermore, large areas of the South, particularly inland South Carolina and Georgia, were relatively inaccessible by land from the North. So even if Washington dared to send men from his army, they probably could not reach the scene of fighting in time to seriously hamper British operations.

However, the key factor that induced the British to completely overhaul their American strategy was the belief that there were vast numbers of loyalists in the South who awaited only the appearance of the king's red-coated soldiers to spur them to take up arms against their rebellious brethren. With the assistance of such loyalist auxiliaries, the South could be subdued and held without the use of large numbers of British regulars.

This impression, based largely on the exaggerated claims of former royal officials and resident loyalists, had little basis in fact. The loyalists were a distinct minority in the South, probably never comprising more than one-third or one-fourth of the region's total population. Later events discouraged even these Tories from playing the active role in the fighting that the British envisioned. But the belief that the loyalists could win the war in the South was so seductive that the king's ministers clung to it long after British officers in America discovered it to be a fallacy.

The first British objective in the South was Savannah, the capital of Georgia, which capitulated in December, 1778. The redcoats then pushed inland, taking Augusta and several other posts. Although constantly harassed by guerrilla raids, the British soon felt secure enough to return their royal governor to administer the colony and to begin boasting that they had taken "the first stripe and star from the rebel flag."

Encouraged by their success in Georgia and the subsequent failure of a Franco-American expedition to retake Savannah, Clinton decided to launch an attack against the South's largest city, the great seaport of Charleston, South Carolina. After a brief siege, Charleston fell to combined British land and naval forces under Clinton's command in May, 1780.

The loss of Charleston and her 5,000 defenders was a stunning blow to the American war effort in the South. The capture of that city gave the British a strong base from which to conduct their operations and an admirable port through which supplies and reinforcements could be funneled to their troops. The surrender of Charleston's 5,000 defenders also eliminated the only large body of organized American troops in the South. The door now seemed open for the redcoats to complete the subjugation of the region.

In June, 1780, Clinton received word that a French fleet was sailing toward the colonies. Assuming the French were headed for New York, and feeling the situation in the South was relatively secure, Clinton decided to return to his northern headquarters.

6   On Clinton's departure, British command in the South passed to
Lord Charles Cornwallis. Over the comng years, the name
Cornwallis would become synonymous with British successes —
and ultimate British defeat — in the South.

Charles Cornwallis was born in 1738, the eldest son of an old,
aristocratic English family. Educated at Eton, he decided before
his eighteenth birthday to become a professional soldier. After
studying for a few months at a military academy in Turin, Italy,
Cornwallis served in Germany with his regiment, the First Grenadier Guards, during the Seven Years' War. The young officer
performed creditably. He entered the war as an ensign and rose to
the rank of lieutenant colonel and regimental commander.

In the summer of 1762, Cornwallis's military career was side-
tracked by the death of his father. Returning to England, he took
his seat in the House of Lords as the Second Earl Cornwallis. He
arrived in London just as Parliament began to enact a series of tax
laws designed to ensure that the colonies would bear a share of the
costs incurred in their defense against the French and their Indian
allies. However, in the face of mounting colonial defiance, these
acts assumed far greater importance as a test of Parliament's
authority to legislate for the colonies. Ironically, in these debates
Cornwallis voted with the Whig minority, which opposed the
attempts of Parliament to dictate to the Americans. In 1765, Earl
Cornwallis voted against the Stamp Act, and, in 1776, he opposed
the passage of the Declaratory Act, which asserted the right of
Parliament to legislate for the colonies "in all cases whatsoever."
However, one of the strongest elements of Cornwallis's character
was his extraordinary sense of loyalty to king and country. So, at
the outbreak of armed rebellion, Cornwallis put aside his personal
opposition to the acts that had precipitated the conflict, and
became one of the first members of the titled nobility to offer his
services for the war in America.

In February, 1776, Cornwallis sailed to America as a major
general commanding 2,500 troops. He arrived in time to join Sir
Henry Clinton's expedition off the mouth of the Cape Fear River,
but played no part in the unsuccessful first attempt to take
Charleston. Returning with Clinton to New York, Cornwallis
joined the main British army and performed capably in its cam-

Lt. Gen. Charles Cornwallis (1738-1805), who later became governor of India, is shown here after being made a marquis in 1792.

paigns in New York and New Jersey. In early 1778, Cornwallis was promoted to lieutenant general. In May of that year, the British commander-in-chief in America, Lord William Howe, resigned and was succeeded by Sir Henry Clinton. Cornwallis was designated as Clinton's successor if the commander-in-chief should in some way become disabled. In this capacity, Cornwallis accompanied the successful expedition against Charleston in 1780, and was given command of British forces in the South when Clinton returned to New York.

At the time of his appointment, Cornwallis was forty-two years old and his health was generally good. The new commander's only physical defect was a blemish in one eye, the result of an injury suffered on the playing fields of Eton. Indeed, Cornwallis's stocky frame gave the impression of considerable personal strength. He would need all of this strength in the months ahead.

On his departure, Clinton left Cornwallis with relatively broad discretionary instructions. He was directed to "constantly regard the safety of Charleston and the tranquility of South Carolina as the principal and indispensable objects of attention." Clinton did not expect this task to be too difficult, as he believed the entire state was on the verge of submission. Peace, in Clinton's opinion, could be assured by establishing a series of strong out-· posts across the up-country and by arming the Palmetto State's loyalists. After assuring the security of South Carolina, Cornwallis was left at liberty to "make a solid move into North Carolina."

While Cornwallis held the South, Clinton hoped to eventually launch operations against the middle colonies. The first step in the plan called for the British to seize bases and recruit loyalists in Virginia. The redcoats would then undertake a giant pincers movement, with troops from Virginia marching north to meet Clinton's forces as they moved down from New York. Thus, the commander-in-chief believed, Washington's army could be trapped and the rebellion effectively crushed. Clinton did not believe he could successfully complete these operations with the 20,000 men he commanded in America, and therefore requested 10,000 more troops and guarantees of continued British naval superiority for the campaign of 1781.

In accordance with Clinton's instructions, Cornwallis constructed a chain of posts at Charleston, Camden, Ninety-Six, Hanging Rock, the Cheraws, and Georgetown. In spite of Clinton's optimistic prediction, this scattering of garrisons failed to secure the peace of the Carolina up-country.

South Carolina had long been torn by fierce partisan warfare. Bands of loyalists had taken up arms around Ninety-Six in 1775, driving rebel partisans to cover. In November, 1775, the rebels received reinforcements from North Carolina and the South Carolina low-country. These forces under Colonels Richard Richardson and William Thompson defeated and scattered the loyalists in a battle at Reedy River. From that time, the loyalists in the South Carolina frontier had been subjected to harassment by rebel partisans supported by the revolutionary government of the province and its militia.

With the British capture of Charleston, the loyalists decided to settle old scores, and opened a campaign of property seizures and house burnings against their old antagonists. Responding to these outrages, newly armed rebel bands gathered and attacked Winnsboro, Fishing Creek, Hanging Rock, and Rocky Mount.

The ferocity of this civil war was attested to by one appalled British officer, Gen. Charles O'Hara, who wrote: "The violence and the passion of these people are beyond every curb of religion, and humanity, they are unbounded and every hour exhibits dreadful wanton mischiefs, murder and violences of every kind unheard of before." Cornwallis himself reported to Clinton on August 6, 1780, that the region between the Pee Dee and Santee rivers was in an "absolute state of rebellion, every friend of [royal] Government has been carried off and his plantation destroyed."

If Cornwallis hoped to secure the tranquility of South Carolina, he obviously had to defeat these rebel partisans. Given the resources at his command, this task proved exceedingly difficult. The marauding guerrilla bands that bedeviled the British in South Carolina were generally mounted, while Cornwallis had few horsemen with his army. When Clinton returned to New York, he took most of the army's cavalry with him, leaving Cornwallis only 300 mounted provincials commanded by Lt. Col. Banastre Tarleton.

Tarleton was an active officer with just the sort of ruthless temperament needed to intimidate the partisans. His admirers in the British army sometimes called him the "Green Dragoon" because of the green uniform coats his men wore, though "Bloody Tarleton" was a more apt characterization for the man whose legionnaires on more than one occasion butchered helpless rebel prisoners. With additional horsemen, "Bloody Tarleton" might have terrorized South Carolina into submission, but he was unequipped to provide adequate coverage for the entire colony.

Cornwallis was personally incapable of the sort of pitiless cruelty that would have cowed the Carolina patriots. Brutality was not a part of his nature, and he realized that such tactics might actually prove counterproductive in the campaign to win the

10   hearts and minds of the disaffected Americans. He did relatively
little to restrain Tarleton's excesses, however, generally praising
the lieutenant colonel in his dispatches and even pressing for his
promotion.

Cornwallis was further hampered because he could not
afford to make wholesale detachments from his army to keep the

*Lt. Col. Banastre Tarleton (1754-1833). Lithograph after portrait
by Sir Joshua Reynolds (1723-92).*

guerrillas at bay. To do so would have been to invite defeat by an American army moving down rapidly from North Carolina.

The capture of Charleston had temporarily removed the threat of a regular American army in the South. However, in early August, 1780, Cornwallis was informed of the approach of Gen. Horatio Gates, the "Hero of Saratoga," and a force consisting of 1,400 Virginia and Maryland Continentals detached from Washington's army, as well as 1,600 North Carolina and Virginia militia. This new threat proved short-lived, for on August 16, 1780, Cornwallis attacked and destroyed Gates's army at Camden, South Carolina.

Cornwallis by this time had become convinced that the best way to insure the security of South Carolina was to invade North Carolina. North Carolina had become a sanctuary and staging ground from which the partisans launched their destructive raids to the south, and the remnant of Gates's army was at that moment being reformed at Hillsborough. The subjugation of North Carolina would therefore eliminate two threats to continued British domination of South Carolina. To Cornwallis's mind, failure to follow this course would inevitably force the British to "give up both South Carolina and Georgia and retire within the walls of Charleston."

One additional consideration was important in leading Cornwallis to his decision to invade North Carolina. North Carolina was widely believed to have one of the largest loyalist populations of all the rebellious colonies. These Tories were widely scattered throughout a thinly populated state and had undergone considerable hardship since their premature rising was crushed at Moore's Creek in 1776. So, in addition to its other military benefits, the subjugation of North Carolina would alleviate the persecution of a sizeable loyalist community whose members, Cornwallis believed, would flock to the king's standard.

Cornwallis planned his invasion of North Carolina for early September, 1780. Leaving 6,000 men to hold the British bases in South Carolina and Georgia, Cornwallis would march with an army of only 2,200 rank and file from Camden, South Carolina, to Charlotte, North Carolina, then to Hillsborough, gathering food and supplies for the winter and recruiting loyalist militia along the way. The left of Cornwallis's column was to be protected by Tory auxiliaries under Maj. Patrick Ferguson, a brilliant but erratic career officer whom Clinton had appointed Inspector of Militia for the Southern Provinces. Ferguson was to move along the eastern edge of the Blue Ridge Mountains, rallying additional loyalist support on the march. He also was to clean out several bands of patriot militia known to be operating from the mountains.

The British began their northern movement on September 9, 1780, but an outbreak of fever in the army forced Cornwallis to delay his advance by two weeks. As a result, he did not reach Charlotte until September 26. Ferguson, meanwhile, established his headquarters at Gilbert Town, North Carolina, and there succeeded in gathering about 1,000 loyalist militia.

From this base, Ferguson issued an ultimatum to the rebel militia — the "over-the-mountain men" — to "desist from their opposition to the British arms" or he would "march his army over the mountains, hang their leaders, and lay their country waste with fire and sword." The over-the-mountain men were a hard lot, toughened by the daily struggle of life on the frontier, and not likely to be intimidated by mere threats of violence. Rather than lay down their arms, 1,000 of these backwoods riflemen gathered at Sycamore Shoals on the Watauga River on September 25, and set out the next day to destroy Ferguson and his Tories.

Realizing that his prey had turned on him, Ferguson withdrew toward the south and the protection of Cornwallis's army. Just across the border into South Carolina, however, Ferguson disregarded his commander's positive orders to avoid an engagement, and turned to meet his pursuers. Ferguson took a position atop Kings Mountain, South Carolina, and there on October 7, 1780, his force was annihilated by the over-the-mountain men. Ferguson and 400 of his loyalists were killed and 600 taken prisoner.

Following their convictions by a drumhead court-martial, nine loyalist leaders were hanged and the remainder marched off to prison. After a brutal march, only 130 prisoners remained to be confined at Hillsborough in November. Although a few died en route, the bulk simply escaped, taking with them tales of their harsh treatment at the hands of the rebels.

A New Commander Rides South

Kings Mountain was a stunning blow to British hopes for the conquest of North Carolina. Not only had Ferguson lost the 1,000 militiamen he had gathered to support Cornwallis's army, but the subsequent brutality of the Whig victors toward their captives dampened the ardor of even the most warlike Tories in the Carolinas. Furthermore, the South Carolina patriots had seized the opportunity afforded by Cornwallis's absence to step up their raids. Almost daily the earl received dispatches telling of partisan outrages against the South Carolina loyalists. As if all this were not enough, fever again broke out among the men of Cornwallis's army. Rather than court further disaster by pushing into an increasingly hostile region with an army decimated by disease, Cornwallis chose to postpone his trouble-plagued invasion of

14   North Carolina, and fell back to Winnsboro, South Carolina.

The same day Cornwallis began his withdrawal from Charlotte, there occurred in New York an event that would have the greatest significance for the future course of the southern campaign. On that Saturday, October 14, 1780, General Washington offered the command of the southern department to Maj. Gen. Nathanael Greene of Rhode Island.

Nathanael Greene was born to Quaker parents in Potowomut, Kent County, Rhode Island, on July 27, 1742. His father, a leader of the Quaker community, was an iron founder. Because he went to work in his father's foundry at an early age, Greene had little formal education. He was, however, a voracious reader, whose taste in literature ran from Greek philosophy to the satires of Jonathan Swift. Greene grew into a formidable man. Standing just under six feet tall, he was stocky, with arms and shoulders made powerful by years of work at the forge. Although blessed with an impressive physique, Greene had two bodily defects. Like his future antagonist, Cornwallis, his right eye was blemished, the result of a smallpox vaccination. A childhood accident also left him with a stiff right knee, which caused him to limp perceptibly.

Greene first became involved in the revolutionary movement in 1768, when he tried to circulate a petition protesting the hated duties imposed by the Townshend Acts of the previous year. Later, he served on the Kent County committee to enforce a boycott of British goods. In 1770, he moved to Coventry, and was elected to represent that village in the Rhode Island general assembly.

Although he was a Quaker, Greene began to take an interest in military affairs following the *Gaspeé* incident in 1772. The *Gaspeé* was a British revenue cutter stationed in Narragansett Bay to enforce Parliament's detested Navigation Acts. In June, 1772, the *Gaspeé* ran aground and was burned by citizens of nearby Providence and Bristol. Since there had been earlier attacks on revenue vessels, the British decided to take a hard line against such acts of vandalism. Orders were issued calling for a commission to investigate the incident and to send those implicated to England for trial. Despite offers of a substantial cash reward for information

*Maj. Gen. Nathanael Greene (1742-86). Mezzotint after
painting by Charles Willson Peale (1741-1827).*

leading to the conviction of the raiders, no suspects were ever
brought to trial. In the course of the investigation, however, an
informant denounced Nathanael Greene as one of the con-
spirators. Greene was outraged by this calumny, and in a most
unpacific manner threatened to put a hole in his accuser big
enough to "let the sun shine through." Recovering his composure,
Greene, like many of his countrymen, came to see the British
response to this incident as a threat to every "lover of liberty in
America."

The first public evidence of this new concern was demon-
strated in the spring of 1773, when Greene attended a large "military gathering" in Plainfield, Connecticut. When the Quaker

Monthly Meeting received a report of his participation in this muster, Greene was given an opportunity to renounce such martial interests. When he refused, he was read out of the Society of Friends.

By the fall of 1774, it was becoming increasingly clear that armed conflict between England and the colonies might be in the offing. Responding to this threat, many volunteer companies, separate from and better trained than the established colonial militia, were raised in New England.

Greene helped organize one such company, the Kentish Guards, at East Greenwich. Because of his role in founding this company, and his obvious knowledge of military science, it came as a shock when he was not elected an officer of the Guards. Greene felt his comrades-in-arms voted against him because they could not bear the indignity of being led by an officer who limped. Although his pride was wounded, Greene shouldered his musket and remained in the Guards as a private.

His knowledge and ability were soon put to good use, however. First, the Rhode Island general assembly elected Greene to its committee to revise the military laws of the province. Still later, following the battles at Lexington and Concord, the legislature selected Greene as its brigadier general to command Rhode Island's 1,500-man Army of Observation in Massachusetts.

Greene joined the forces in Massachusetts in time for the siege of Boston, where his skill and knowledge were sources of universal admiration. In June, 1775, when Congress adopted the Continental Army, Greene was commissioned a brigadier general. Two months later, he was promoted to the rank of major general.

Perhaps Greene's most ardent admirer in the Continental Army was Gen. George Washington, and Greene rapidly became the commander-in-chief's most trusted subordinate. It soon became common knowledge that Washington had designated Greene as his successor should he, for any reason, be unable to continue as commander-in-chief.

In March, 1778, following the horrors of the winter at Valley Forge, Washington asked Greene to assume the office of quartermaster general and bring order to the army's chaotic supply system. He accepted and performed this difficult assignment with consummate skill. However, the methods Greene employed as quartermaster general were not above reproach. There is, for instance, evidence that his department regularly did business with companies in which Greene's relatives had a financial interest. Such arrangements inevitably made the quartermaster general the object of considerable congressional criticism. After much wrangling with Congress, Greene resigned his position in July, 1780, and was given command of the strategically important post at West Point, New York.

Following the disaster at Camden in August, 1780, Congress directed General Washington to choose a successor for the disgraced Horatio Gates. The commander-in-chief unhesitatingly selected Nathanael Greene. At this time, a leader of Greene's experience, both as a combat officer and as an administrator, was sorely needed in the South, for the new commander would face problems that others might have considered insurmountable.

The British had some 8,000 men in South Carolina and Georgia in late 1780. These redcoats had captured 5,000 Americans at Charleston and all but destroyed a second rebel army at Camden. At best, Greene could hope to find only 2,000 men under arms in his new command. From reports he had received, Greene knew these men were poorly clothed, armed, and equipped.

As he rode south, Greene stopped in Philadelphia, where he sought weapons and supplies for his army from both Congress and the state of Pennsylvania. As he continued his journey, he made similar requests of the governors of Maryland and Virginia. Although his appeals were answered with assurances of support, Greene doubted that these promises would be kept. "They all promised fair," Greene wrote, "but I fear will do little; ability is wanting in some, and inclination in others."

Greene assumed command of the southern department at the army's winter encampment near Charlotte, North Carolina, on December 3, 1780. To his horror, he found conditions were even worse than he had expected. The men were poorly fed, wretchedly clothed, and miserably equipped. The combination of poor diet and inadequate winter clothing had led to epidemic outbreaks of diarrhea, dysentery, and other ailments which had incapacitated about half of the troops. Although the army's rolls carried the names of 2,307 men, Greene probably could have mustered no more than 800 healthy, properly clothed and equipped soldiers for battle. As Greene tersely concluded, his new command was "but the shadow of an army in the midst of distress."

Greene at once set to work to relieve the suffering of his men. Within a few days, he decided the army could not remain at Charlotte. Rations were in critically short supply because the British had swept the region of provisions prior to their withdrawal in October. The new commander sent scouting parties south to find areas where food was more abundant. After inspecting the army's uniforms, Greene concluded that a number of the Virginia troops were so wretchedly clad that they could be of no possible service in the coming campaign. These men were sent home, and Greene penned a sharp note to Gov. Thomas Jefferson, protesting that "no man will think himself bound to fight the battle of a State that leaves him to perish for want of covering."

The general then ordered that all sheeting material and osnaburg (coarse linen cloth) that could be collected in the area be sent to Salisbury, North Carolina, to be sewn into overalls to cover the ragged warriors who remained. He further directed that hides be collected and dispatched to Salem, where Moravian craftsmen would fashion shoes for the army. Greene also sought to provide arms and ammunition for the coming campaign from a number of sources.

Around the middle of December, scouts reported that food supplies were plentiful in an area along the Pee Dee River in South Carolina. In light of this intelligence, Greene decided at once to move half of his army about 75 miles southeast to Cheraw, near the falls of the Pee Dee. The remainder of his command, 1,000 Maryland and Delaware Continentals and some militia units under the command of Brig. Gen. Daniel Morgan, would ford the Catawba River and rendezvous in South Carolina with partisans under the command of Col. Thomas Sumter. There Morgan would rally the patriots, gather supplies, and threaten the redcoats' western flank. Greene knew that this disposition would

Brig. Gen. Daniel Morgan (1736-1802). Engraving by J.F.E. Prud'homme (1800-92), based on a sketch by John Trumbull.

have an unsettling effect on the British commander, Lord Cornwallis.

[I]t compels my adversary to divide his [army] and holds him in doubt as to his own line of conduct. He cannot leave Morgan behind him to come at me, or his posts of Ninety-Six and Augusta would be exposed. And he cannot chase Morgan far or prosecute his views upon Virginia, while I am here with the whole country open before me. I am as near Charleston as he is.

Just as Greene anticipated, Cornwallis divided his army to deal with these threats. Lt. Col. Banastre Tarleton was dispatched with his provincial cavalry and all of the army's light troops—highly mobile infantrymen or riflemen used principally as skirmishers—to hunt down and destroy Morgan. This dispersal of his forces left Cornwallis with only 900 men, but 1,500 additional troops under the command of Maj. Gen. Alexander Leslie were expected to arrive soon from Virginia. After Morgan was eliminated, Cornwallis could unite all of his forces and destroy Greene's main army at his leisure.

Cornwallis felt no particular concern for the safety of Tarleton's expedition. The "Green Dragoon" was an experienced officer directing 1,150 of the British army's finest troops against a numerically inferior foe. Yet on January 17, 1781, Tarleton impetuously rode into a trap at a place called Hannah's Cowpens near Broad River, losing all but a handful of his men to Morgan. Cornwallis, stunned by the loss of his light troops, wrote dejectedly of the Battle of Cowpens: "The late affair has almost broke my heart."

Race to the Dan

As TARLETON and the remnants of his shattered command limped back to Lord Cornwallis's camp at Turkey Creek, 30 miles from Cowpens, the British commander faced a pivotal decision: Should he pursue Morgan's victorious forces as they fell back into North Carolina or should he withdraw his men to the security of their bases in South Carolina? Prudence clearly dictated that he follow the latter course.

The months of late fall and early winter 1780–1781 had been extremely hard for the British troops in the South. In October, the redcoats had been beset by fever which, for a time, debilitated even Lord Cornwallis. As fall turned to winter, food supplies dwindled. Although British commissaries scoured the countryside for provisions, they could not obtain sufficient supplies to fill the army's larders. Nor could they procure horses and wagons to haul the scanty rations that were available. Even more serious, in the span of four months the British and their loyalist allies had been defeated in two major engagements, losing upwards of 2,000 men while inflicting negligible casualties on the Americans.

Judging by the difficulties his army had experienced, Cornwallis would have been well advised to return to Charleston, where his army could safely recuperate and he could consider future plans. But Cornwallis was a pugnacious soldier, so aggressive that he was dubbed the "modern Hannibal" by Nathanael Greene. Having been bloodied, the earl's natural inclination was to strike back at his tormentors. He decided to pursue and destroy Morgan.

This decision was based on more than Cornwallis's sheer intractability. The keystone of the British strategy in the South was the assumption that the region could be subjugated only if resident loyalists rose up and aided in the suppression of the rebellion. Realistically, the British could hope to retain Tory support only as long as the people believed in the invincibility of the king's red-coated troops. The capture of Charleston and the American defeat at Camden had convinced many Tories that the revolution could not succeed and that they could take up arms without fear of reprisals by their disaffected countrymen.

Kings Mountain was a blow to loyalist recruiting, but it probably did not adversely affect British military prestige for, with the exception of Ferguson himself, no regular troops had been engaged. Cowpens was a different matter. A mixed American army of Continentals and militiamen had faced and soundly beaten a force of crack redcoats in open battle. Cornwallis determined that the only way to mitigate this defeat and restore faith in the superiority of British arms was to crush Morgan.

An additional factor weighed heavily in Cornwallis's decision to assume the offensive. Illness and battle losses had begun to take a serious toll of British manpower. Tarleton had lost 900 men at Cowpens, among them 600 unwounded prisoners of war. If he could overtake Morgan and liberate these captives, Cornwallis would appreciably strengthen his army.

On January 18, 1781, Cornwallis received enough reinforcements to begin his pursuit of Morgan. That day the remnants of Tarleton's command, some 200 men, straggled into camp. More important, the 1,500 redcoats under Maj. Gen. Alexander Leslie also arrived.

The latter was part of a larger force of 2,500 men sent to the Chesapeake region of Virginia in October, 1780, by Sir Henry Clinton. Clinton intended for these troops to destroy supplies destined for Greene's army and to divert American attention from Cornwallis's offensive in the Carolinas. The commander-in-chief also meant for Leslie's forces to unite with those of Cornwallis when the earl's army eventually reached Virginia. However, Cornwallis believed that he needed additional manpower for his projected reinvasion of North Carolina, and therefore ordered Leslie to ship his men to Charleston.

Responsibility for continuing the harassment of the patriots in Virginia shifted to Brig. Gen. Benedict Arnold, who sailed from New York with 1,600 men on December 20, 1780. Leslie landed at Charleston on December 16, 1780, and a few days later marched with 1,500 men to Camden. On January 9, 1781, Cornwallis ordered Leslie to join his main army.

With these additions, Cornwallis's army numbered 2,400 men. But the British general lost almost two days awaiting the arrival of these reinforcements. By the time his army began marching north, Morgan was well beyond Broad River. The British moved quickly, but wasted more time when they missed the road Cornwallis wished them to take. By the time this error was corrected, Morgan had crossed the Catawba, three hours ahead of the panting redcoats. Cornwallis then pushed on to the east, reaching Ramsour's Mill on the Little Catawba on January 25. There, to his consternation, he found that winter rains had flooded the river, making it impossible to ford. Likewise, the area's miserable dirt roads had been transformed into quagmires.

On these muddy thoroughfares, Cornwallis could not hope to overtake the fleeing Americans and so paused at Ramsour's Mill to allow his men to forage and to give himself time to consider his options. The earl concluded that the best way to speed the movement of his column was to eliminate all but its most essential baggage. He ordered all of the army's wagons burned, beginning with his own. Only those vehicles that carried salt, ammunition, or hospital stores were spared from the flames. His army's burden lightened, Cornwallis moved out on January 27, for Beattie's Ford on the Catawba. Morgan, meanwhile, was camped on the other side of the river at Sherrill's Ford.

On receiving news of the Battle of Cowpens, Nathanael Greene at once decided to reunite his forces. To that end, he directed Gen. Isaac Huger of South Carolina to lead the regiments on the Pee Dee to Salisbury, where they would await the arrival of Morgan's troops. He further intended, if sufficient militia should come out, to offer Lord Cornwallis battle. Therefore, he issued calls to Congress and the states of Virginia and North Carolina for men to strengthen his army. As for himself, Greene intended to ride the 80 miles to Sherrill's Ford where he would personally direct the retreat of Morgan's light troops.

Greene arrived at Morgan's camp on January 30. He was immensely gratified that Morgan had complied with an earlier order to convey all the prisoners captured at Cowpens to Virginia, where they would be out of Cornwallis's reach. The commanding general was less satisfied with the poor response to his pleas for militia to join his army. Even more serious, most of the Virginia militia that had fought at Cowpens left the army because their enlistments had expired. They were joined on their homeward journey by most of the Virginians from Huger's command.

His appeals for aid unanswered, Greene decided to continue the retreat Morgan had begun. He ordered all the army's stores removed to Guilford Courthouse, some 30 miles south of the Virginia border, and authorized Morgan to seize all civilian horses and wagons needed to accomplish this task. The supplies safely dispatched, Morgan marched his command toward Salisbury on the night of January 31.

Cornwallis, meanwhile, had been delayed two days while he waited for the swollen Catawba River to fall. Finally, at dawn on February 1, the British crossed the river at McCowan's Ford. This crossing was contested for a time by 300 North Carolina militia under Gen. William Lee Davidson. In a short exchange of musketry, the Carolinians inflicted about 35 casualties on the British. When General Davidson was killed, his men fled.

His troops over the Catawba, Cornwallis pressed the pursuit of his adversary. Morgan by this time had opened a 30-mile lead over the British, but the "modern Hannibal" was not daunted. Cornwallis made up ground rapidly, covering more than 20 miles each day. Cold winter rains continued to fall, encouraging the British general to believe that he could trap the fleeing Americans against the banks of the flooded Yadkin River. He was disappointed when the advance elements of his army reached Trading Ford on the Yadkin and found that the Americans had crossed the swollen river on boats that Greene had ordered collected from the surrounding area. With this tiny armada, Greene had successfully evacuated all of Morgan's army, its supplies, and a number of civilian refugees as well. Unable to follow, Cornwallis vented his frustration by ordering his artillery to shell the American camp on the far shore.

While British cannon balls rained harmlessly around the American camp, General Greene busily wrote dispatches. The most important of these ordered General Huger to rendezvous with Morgan's forces at Guilford Courthouse. The commanders of the North Carolina militia also were directed to muster their troops at Guilford. He also commanded that guns, flints, ammunition, and other supplies the army would need in battle be collected at the courthouse. All other stores were to be sent across the Dan River into Virginia.

Although he was disappointed by the escape of his prey, Cornwallis still believed he could overtake and defeat Greene and Morgan. Convinced that Greene could not find enough boats to repeat his Yadkin River miracle, the British general determined to move up the Yadkin to Shallow Ford, cross, and cut the Americans off from the fords of the Dan.

Cornwallis forded the Yadkin on February 8, the same day that Huger rendezvoused with Greene and Morgan at Guilford Courthouse, 25 miles away. While his troops rested, Greene pondered his next steps. Only 200 militia had mustered at Guilford. Furthermore, Huger's troops from the Pee Dee were in wretched shape as a result of their "nakedness, the want of powder, poor horses, broken harness, and bad roads on the march." At a council of war, it was decided that the American army was not yet strong enough to face Cornwallis's determined veterans. Greene elected

26 once again to divide his army, sending a body of 700 light troops—infantry, cavalry, and riflemen—northwest toward the upper fords of the Dan. These troops were to be commanded by the army's adjutant general, Col. Otho H. Williams of Maryland, an excellent officer with a brilliant combat record. Williams was to replace Daniel Morgan, who was so painfully afflicted by rheumatism and other ailments that he had been forced to return to his home in Virginia. Greene, meanwhile, would march the bulk of the army 70 miles northeast and ford the Dan at Boyd's and Irwin's ferries. The army's quartermaster, Edward Carrington, had been sent ahead to secure boats for crossing at these points.

Greene and Williams moved from Guilford Courthouse on February 10, with the British barely 40 miles behind. Even by the wretched standards of the southern campaign, this was an exceedingly difficult march. Rain fell almost constantly and the roads, churned and rutted by the army's transit, became almost impassable. The combination of cold, rain, mud, and inadequate clothing was brutal for enlisted men and officers alike.

One bitter night, Greene and South Carolina Governor John Rutledge, who had joined the army after the fall of Charleston, sought shelter in an abandoned shack. The two leaders piled onto the remains of a bed and soon were asleep. They were awakened late in the night by the rude kicking of a hog that had crawled into their bunk to escape the cold and rain.

Cornwallis was at first deceived by Greene's feint, following Williams toward the upper fords of the Dan. When he discovered the American commander's true intention, the British column veered toward Irwin's Ferry. Williams responded by placing his light troops between the two armies, staying just ahead of the British, destroying bridges and generally impeding their pursuit. The redcoats sometimes came within sight of Williams's rear guard, but never could catch up, and Tarleton's cavalry was held at bay by American horsemen under William Washington and Henry "Light Horse Harry" Lee. Meanwhile, Greene's army crossed the flooded Dan at Irwin's Ferry on February 14, and Williams followed shortly at Boyd's.

A few hours after the last of Williams's troops rowed across the Dan, the flooded river began to fall. Greene at first believed that the British surely would follow, and was determined to retreat further into Virginia if necessary. Lord Cornwallis had had enough of this seemingly endless chase, however. His men and their food supplies had been exhausted by their long, hard marches. Ahead lay the prospect of desperate fighting against Greene's united forces in the largest, wealthiest, and most populous of the rebellious colonies. So, after giving his troops a day's rest, the British commander retired to Hillsborough, North Carolina, to gather provisions and rally loyalist support.

Greene's handling of the retreat from North Carolina was brilliantly conceived and masterfully executed. Although the American general had temporarily ceded control of still another southern state to the British, he had kept his army intact and saved its supplies, all the while drawing the enemy deeper into hostile territory.

Although he was the object of some criticism for abandoning North Carolina without a fight, Greene was unconcerned. He realized that two American armies had already been destroyed in the South. Hence his command was a precious, perhaps irreplaceable, resource, whose preservation was more important than any momentary popularity won in an ill-advised battle. He had long ago come to the conclusion that the American army in the South should fight only under the most favorable circumstances. As he had counseled Morgan prior to Cowpens, Greene knew that American generals must be impervious to criticism, always looking "to the long side of the struggle." He would shortly demonstrate that, when circumstances were to his liking, he was not afraid to fight the British.

Watching and Waiting

GREENE ESTABLISHED his headquarters at Halifax Courthouse near the Dan River and once again began the familiar task of seeking supplies and reinforcements. This time his appeals for troops did not go unheeded. Reports soon came in that men were joining Generals John Butler and Robert Lawson as well as other militia officers in North Carolina. A few days later, 800 Virginia militia under Gen. Edward Stevens arrived in camp, followed shortly by news that detachments of riflemen led by Charles Lynch and William Campbell, the "hero of Kings Mountain," were also en route.

Cornwallis, meantime, was enjoying less success at Hillsborough. Hoping that Greene's retreat from North Carolina would inspire the area's Tories, Cornwallis erected the "King's Standard" and invited "all His Majesty's loving Subjects to take up arms and join in defense of their civil liberties." This proclamation brought forth many pledges of support, but few enlistments.

Likewise, Hillsborough and its vicinity yielded negligible quantities of supplies. American troops had often used this town as a base and had done a thorough job of stripping the region of provisions. Within a few days, the British troops hungrily devoured all the food they found on hand. When the redcoats then began to butcher farmers' draft animals, local support for the British began a noticeable decline.

British hopes for encouraging Tory support were dealt a virtual death blow in late February. General Greene, at his headquarters in Virginia, was anxious to reestablish an American presence in North Carolina, both to hamper British efforts to recruit loyalists and to inspire the state's patriots to take up arms.

Greene began to dispatch units of his army back across the Dan on February 18. The first such troops sent back into North Carolina were a body of militia under Brig. Gen. Andrew Pickens, the famous South Carolina partisan, and the cavalry and light infantry of "Light Horse Harry" Lee's legion. Greene instructed Pickens and Lee to hover about Cornwallis's camp, interrupting British communications and disrupting their efforts to forage and recruit loyalists.

At about this same time, Cornwallis was informed that 300 Tory militiamen, assembled by Col. John Pyle in the area between the Haw and the Deep rivers, were marching to Hillsborough. Encouraged by this report, the British general directed Colonel Tarleton to take his cavalry and escort these loyalists into camp. Unfortunately for these friends of the king, Lee and Pickens reached the Tories before Tarleton's men. Pyle initially mistook the youthful Colonel Lee for Tarleton, and discovered his error too late to escape disaster. Only a handful of Tories survived the massacre, which came to be known as "Pyle's Hacking Match."

A few days later, another loyalist band was destroyed because of a similar case of mistaken identity. This time Tarleton intercepted a group of about 70 Tories from Rowan County

bound for Cornwallis's camp. "Bloody Tarleton" incorrectly iden-
tified these loyalists as rebels and attacked, killing four and
wounding thirty. With his troops stripping the countryside of
food and livestock, and killing more of their friends than enemies,
it is not surprising that Lord Cornwallis's hopes for Tory support
were largely disappointed.

After sending Pickens and Lee into North Carolina, Greene
on February 20 dispatched his light troops under Colonel Williams back across the Dan. Greene followed on February 24 with
the remainder of his Continentals and 600 to 700 Virginia militia
commanded by Brig. Gen. Edward Stevens. If enough North
Carolina militia joined him, the American commander was determined to attack Cornwallis. Shortly after fording the Dan,
Greene was encouraged by the arrival of 260 riflemen under Colonels Hugh Crockett and William Campbell. Yet even with these
additions, he did not feel his army was strong enough to face
Cornwallis's veterans. Greene reluctantly decided to await still
more reinforcements.

Informed of Greene's return to North Carolina, Cornwallis
broke camp at Hillsborough on February 25. Fording Haw River,
he moved to a position on Stinking Quarter Creek, a tributary of
Alamance Creek. From this central location, the British could
control the roads leading to Salisbury, Guilford Courthouse,
High Rock Ford on Haw River, and Hillsborough.

Greene marched west and crossed Haw River at High Rock
Ford on February 26, camping for the night on the road leading to
Guilford Courthouse. The following day, he joined Williams,
Lee, and Pickens, and moved his army south to the region bounded by Reedy Fork and Troublesome Creeks, about 15 miles from
Cornwallis's camp. From this position, Greene advanced his light
troops to harry the redcoats. On March 1, Williams camped three
miles from the British on the old Alamance battleground. The
next day Lee skirmished inconclusively with Tarleton's cavalry
nearby.

The constant harassment of his army was a source of considerable difficulty for Lord Cornwallis. British food supplies, never
plentiful, became increasingly scarce. Sgt. Roger Lamb of the
Royal Welch Fusiliers reflected with marked distaste on the redcoats' skimpy fare.

Sometimes we had turnips served out for food when we came to a turnip field; or arriving at a field of corn, we converted our canteens into rasps and ground our Indian corn for bread; when we could get no Indian corn, we were compelled to eat liver as a substitute for bread, with our lean beef.

Poor diet and constant exposure to the elements led to renewed outbreaks of camp fever, which weakened the army and made life dreary for Cornwallis's troops. An equally serious problem for the British commander was the mounting toll of casualties suffered in skirmishes with the Americans. In February, the British army lost a total of 227 soldiers either killed or wounded in brushes with Greene's troops or disabled by illness. Studying these figures, Cornwallis knew he must soon defeat the Americans in battle or see his own army crippled by attrition.

But Greene was not yet ready to risk a general engagement. Indeed, the American commander faced serious problems of his own. Like their red-coated counterparts, American officers experienced considerable difficulty in finding enough food for their men. Many, if not most, of the militiamen who had joined Greene's army had arrived on horseback, and their horses gobbled up fodder sorely needed for the army's cavalry mounts and draft animals. To relieve the pressure on his commissaries, Greene ordered 1,000 of these militia horses sent away from the army. To the American general's dismay, however, many of the undisciplined militiamen refused to part with their mounts and simply rode home.

On March 6, Cornwallis attempted to bring about the general engagement he so badly wanted. Noting that the Americans "were posted carelessly at separate Plantations for the convenience of subsisting," the British commander, under cover of early morning fog, threw his forces across Alamance Creek and marched rapidly toward Wetzell's (Whitesell's) Mill on the Reedy Fork. Cornwallis hoped to cut off Williams's light troops south of the Haw from the main American army, thereby forcing Greene to come to the aid of this isolated detachment.

Greene was not deceived by this ploy, and directed Williams to fall back. Williams crossed his main body over the Reedy Fork at Wetzell's Mill, detaching a rear guard of riflemen under Colonels William Preston and William Campbell and Lee's cavalry to

32 cover his retreat. After a sharp action, described by one militiaman as "a smart skirmish, in which a great many Tories were sent to the lower region," British troops under Lt. Col. James Webster pushed across the creek and pursued the retreating Americans for a mile before abandoning the chase. Williams halted about five miles from Wetzell's Mill, where he received instructions to cross his command over to the north side of Haw River.

Greene elected to keep his army north of the Haw while he awaited the arrival of additional militia units. Reinforcements were more sorely needed than ever, for shortly after Wetzell's Mill, Greene was obliged to send Pickens's South Carolina and Georgia militia back south. The Georgians and South Carolinians had begun to grumble loudly that they had been sacrificed at Wetzell's Mill to protect the Continentals. They also complained that after months of service their clothing was tattered, leaving them cruelly exposed to the elements. Greene concluded that under these circumstances it would be best to send the men back to South Carolina, where they might replace their ragged apparel and cooperate with partisan operations against the British outposts.

While he waited north of Haw River, Greene worried that the redcoats might not allow him the time he needed to gather his reinforcements. To confuse the British as to his whereabouts, the American commander changed his campsite each night, telling no one in advance where the army would bivouac. The Wetzell's Mill experience suggested that Cornwallis favored the early morning hours for surprise attacks, so Greene was up before dawn each morning, personally inspecting the army's sentries and watching for signs of enemy activity. The commanding general's vigilance was unquestionably a source of inspiration for his men. On one of his dawn inspections, the general was distracted by the particularly raucous snoring of Col. John Greene (no relation) of Virginia. Asked how he could sleep so soundly when the enemy was near, Col. Greene replied, "Why General, I knew that you were awake."

Fighting on New Garden Road

Around March 10, Greene's long wait was ended by the arrival of his last reinforcements. Brigadier General Lawson led 1,000 Virginia militia into camp, shortly followed by 1,000 more citizen soldiers commanded by Brigadier Generals John Butler and Thomas Eaton of North Carolina. Virginia eighteen-month Continentals numbering 530 also joined the army, as did a few more riflemen from western North Carolina and Virginia. With these additions, Greene now had under his command an army of approximately 4,400 men to face Cornwallis's 2,200 redcoats.

On paper, at least, the sheer size of this force gave the American commander a huge advantage over his British counterpart. The odds were narrowed considerably, however, by the quality of

Cornwallis's troops. These redcoats were well-disciplined veterans, tempered in the fires of scores of battles and skirmishes, and toughened by their long marches across the Carolinas. Less than half of Greene's army (his 1,490 Continentals and some of the militia) had seen action against the British, and no one could predict how the inexperienced men would perform in battle. On the other hand, Greene knew that his army was now as strong as it was ever likely to be. To delay further would allow short-term militia enlistments to expire, and would invite desertions of men who might rather spend their time preparing their farms for spring planting than sitting idly in army camps. After weighing the alternatives, the American commander decided to strike the enemy.

The next few days were filled with activity as Greene made his preparations for battle. Badly needed supplies were distributed, and the troops were directed to cook two days' rations. Williams's light infantry corps was disbanded and its men dispersed throughout the army. March 13 was devoted to drilling the raw militia levies, and to instructing them in the technique of firing volleys by platoons and battalions. Even for experienced riflemen, the discipline required to fire en masse did not come easily, and the casualty toll for this day of basic training included one man shot through the head and another wounded by a ricocheting musket ball. These tasks completed, the American army broke its camp at Speedwell Ironworks on Troublesome Creek at 6 A.M. on March 14, and marched south toward Guilford Courthouse.

The men in the ranks knew a battle was imminent and their morale was excellent. St. George Tucker, a Virginian serving in Lawson's militia, wrote to his wife, "[We] are this moment marching to attack Cornwallis with a force which I am in hopes is full able to cope with him."

The army reached Guilford that afternoon and pitched camp for the night. From Guilford Courthouse, the Americans were within easy striking distance of the British, who were bivouacked at Deep River Friends Meeting House, 12 miles to the southwest. This was no accident, for Greene meant to attack the enemy the next morning.

In the evening of March 14, Lord Cornwallis received confirmation of earlier reports that Greene's army was encamped at Guilford Courthouse. This intelligence delighted the British general. After months of chasing a foe who was as elusive as a wisp of smoke, it appeared that the Americans would at last stand and fight.

Cornwallis was far too agressive to sit docilely in his camp and await Nathanael Greene, and so decided to attack the Americans. By a rapid march—and a bit of good luck—he hoped to surprise the rebels in their camp. His men would be outnumbered more than two to one by the enemy, but the redcoats were accustomed to fighting against long odds in America. The earl put his trust in the skill and discipline of the British soldier, which had been proved so often on battlefields in both Europe and America.

While his men drew ammunition and inspected their arms, Cornwallis laid his plans for the next day. The army's baggage train, escorted by 120 regulars and Lieutenant Colonel Hamilton's loyalist regiment, would march that night to Bell's Mill on Deep River. The remainder of the army, just under 2,000 men, would move out on New Garden Road (Salisbury Road) toward Guilford Courthouse at 5:30 the following morning.

While Cornwallis made his preparations for battle, Nathanael Greene was spending a restless night. To protect his army against surprise attack, Greene directed "Light Horse Harry" Lee to take his legion (one company of cavalry numbering 75 men, a battalion of 82 infantrymen, and about 100 Virginia riflemen under Col. William Campbell) and camp on New Garden Road, two to three miles west of Guilford Courthouse. Lee, in turn, dispatched Lt. James Heard with a few horsemen to "place himself near the British camp, and to report from time to time such occurences as might happen." Around 2 A.M., Heard sent word to Lee that there was considerable movement around the enemy encampment. Lee directed Heard to move along the British flank to determine if Cornwallis's whole army was in motion. Although this reconnaisance was hampered by patrols ranging far from the redcoats' lines, Heard reported to Lee at 4 A.M. that the rumbling of wagon wheels could be heard, indicating that a "general movement" was underway. In fact, what

Heard interpreted as evidence of a general movement was the British baggage train moving out for Bell's Mills. Nonetheless, Lee conveyed Heard's message to Greene. He also ordered his troopers called to arms and directed them to "take breakfast as quickly as possible."

Just as Lee's men finished their meal, a courier rode into camp bearing a message from Greene. Unwilling to act until he was certain that the whole British army was in motion, the commanding general directed Lee to proceed with his entire command, ride down all obstructions, and ascertain the truth. The athletic young colonel called his dragoons to horse at once and led them west along New Garden Road. The infantrymen, regulars and militia, were directed to follow as rapidly as possible.

As Lee's horsemen galloped off, the advance elements of Cornwallis's army were nearing New Garden Meeting House. At the head of the column rode Banastre Tarleton. Like a hunter's hound, Tarleton's was to seek out the enemy, and, if necessary, hold him at bay until Cornwallis's main army could arrive for the kill. For this purpose the "Green Dragoon" had at his disposal about 500 men, including his personal command, the 272 loyalist cavalrymen and infantrymen of the British legion. The balance of his detachment was composed of 84 jaegers (German riflemen) and more than 100 light infantrymen of the Brigade of Guards.

Seven miles out from their camp, Tarleton's cavalry and foot soldiers approached New Garden Meeting House. Clattering past the Quaker house of worship, the redcoats suddenly were greeted by a ragged volley of carbine and pistol shots, fired by Lieutenant Heard's pickets. As Tarleton's troopers returned his fire, the American dragoons cantered away.

Heard met Lee about four miles west of Guilford Courthouse and reported that the redcoats were approaching in force. Lee elected to fall back closer to his trailing infantry supports and, not coincidentally, to the main American army. Tarleton, impetuous as ever, saw this tactical withdrawal but mistakenly interpreted it as a "rout" and ordered his men to press forward. The rear of Lee's column was covered by a troop of dragoons commanded by a Captain Armstrong, and these veteran troopers beat back this first British assault. While Tarleton reformed his horsemen for a second charge, Lee's dragoons entered a section of the highway described by their commander as a "long lane with high curved fences on either side of the road." In such cramped quarters, Tarleton would be unable to deploy his force to good advantage. Lee cunningly allowed the British legionnaires to press tightly into this narrow alley before ordering his men to wheel about and charge their pursuers. As Lee later recalled, the effect of this unexpected attack was devastating.

The whole of the enemy's section was dismounted, and many of the horses prostrated; some of the [British] dragoons killed, the rest made prisoner; not a single American soldier or horse was injured. Tarleton retired with celerity.

Lt. Col. Henry Lee (1756-1818). This 1862 engraving is after a painting by Alonzo Chappel that probably owes facial details to one by Gilbert Stuart (1755-1828).

Bested in this encounter, Tarleton's provincials galloped back toward New Garden, with Lee's men close behind. Hoping to reach his infantry supports before he could be overtaken by the American cavalry, the "Green Dragoon" led his men down an obscure path running southeast from the main road. Lee, equally intent on preventing this junction of British forces, "followed the common route by the Quaker Meeting-house."

"Light Horse Harry's" plan failed, however, because the trailing British and German foot soldiers were much closer than he had anticipated. As his troopers approached New Garden Meeting House, they unexpectedly encountered the leading redcoat infantry units. Lee recalled (referring to himself in the third person):

As Lee, with his column in full speed, got up to the meeting-house, the British guards had just reached it, displaying [deploying] in a moment, [they] gave the American cavalry a close general fire.

In the confusion that followed, Lee was thrown from his horse, but remounted and ordered his cavalry to retreat. As his horsemen fell back, the infantry of Lee's legion reached the front at a dead run, soon followed by Campbell's riflemen. These winded but able foot soldiers opened fire at once on the advancing Guards. In Lee's words, "the action became sharp and was bravely maintained on both sides."

This skirmish lasted for about half an hour, until the arrival of additional British units convinced Lee that Cornwallis's whole army would soon be on hand. "Light Horse Harry" then ordered his detachment to retire toward Guilford Courthouse, his cavalry covering the column's rear.

Falling back about a mile to an unnamed crossroads, the Americans paused once again to check their pursuers. The fighting here was the heaviest of the morning, as more units of the main British army arrived on the scene and were pushed into action. Cornwallis himself may have reached the front by this time to direct the engagement. So heavy was the fighting that the din of gunfire could be clearly heard by Greene's troops three miles away. Lee had no hope of holding off the bulk of Cornwallis's army indefinitely. When the Royal Welch Fusiliers joined the struggle, he ordered his men to retreat, the American horsemen reaching Greene's lines shortly before noon.

Tarleton estimated his losses in the heavy skirmishes around New Garden as 30 killed and wounded. Lee claimed American casualties were much lighter. Losses, however, were particularly heavy among the officers of both sides. Capt. James Tate of the Virginia militia and Lt. Jonathan Snowden of Lee's legion fell. Among the British, Captains Goodrick and Schutz of the guards and Lt. Ernst von Trott of the Hessian von Bose Regiment died, and Colonel Tarleton lost the index and middle fingers of his right hand to an American musket ball.

Most maps of the battle depend on this one, published in Banastre Tarleton's account of southern campaigns of 1780 and 1781. For proper orientation the north point should be rotated left 50°.

"A Wilderness Covered
with Tall Woods"

Greene used to good advantage the time bought for him by Lee's delaying actions. It is not clear exactly when the American general received positive confirmation of the British army's advance, but his orders to Lee suggest that Greene suspected the truth as early as 4 A.M. At any rate, Greene was awake and active at an early hour. His hopes for attacking Cornwallis were now forgotten, as the troops had to be fed and then quickly placed in lines of battle to repel the imminent British assault.

Fortunately, Greene was familiar with this region. He had first seen Guilford Courthouse in November, 1780, as he rode toward Charlotte to take command of the southern army. At that time, the area's terrain had favorably impressed him as a potential battle site. Following Cowpens, Geene designated Guilford as the rendezvous point for the two wings of his army, and undoubtedly would have faced the enemy then had more militia reinforcements joined his forces. A little more than a month later, Greene had 4,400 men on ground which was to his liking. Now he needed a battle plan.

Eighteenth-century warfare seems a strangely formalized affair to the modern observer. Common sense rebels at the characteristic picture of long ranks of soldiers in brightly colored uniforms standing shoulder-to-shoulder on open fields, firing at similar masses of enemy troops. In fact, such apparently suicidal tactics were dictated by the limitations of the period's firearms.

The standard infantry weapon of both the British and American armies in the Revolutionary War was the flintlock musket. Because the musket was smooth-bored, it was wildly inaccurate, particularly at ranges greater than 100 yards. Since no officer could rely on the marksmanship of his troops, the accepted tactics of the period called for the arrangement of scores of men in tight lines, firing their weapons in volleys. Although individually untrustworthy, a number of muskets discharged at the same time, and in the same general direction, could inflict substantial damage.

Few engagements were decided simply by exchanges of gunfire, however. The true queen of battle was the bayonet, a foot-long triangular steel blade that fitted onto the musket barrel, transforming the firearm into a six-foot-long pike. At close range, the bayonet was brutally effective. Furthermore, it was a potent psychological weapon. Considerable discipline and courage were required for a man to hold his ground as a sea of bayonets swept toward him.

The British were well aware of the bloody virtues of the bayonet, and the red-coated infantrymen were rigorously trained in its use. It was largely their skill with this weapon that allowed British troops to inflict a long series of defeats on American armies early in the war. By the sixth year of the conflict, however, many Continental regiments had received enough training and had gained sufficient battlefield experience to enable them to fight on equal terms with the best British units.

The same could not be said for the American militia. These citizen soldiers generally had little discipline, training, or combat experience to prepare them for the horrors of battle. Furthermore, the militiamen were armed with their personal weapons, an odd collection of old muskets, rifles, and fowling pieces. Many did not have bayonets; indeed, civilian weapons were not designed to accomodate them. So a raw militiaman sent into battle against British regulars, with little preparation and lacking even a bayonet for self protection, was at a decided disadvantage. It is little wonder, then, that the militia often behaved poorly in battle. At Camden, for instance, Virginia militia units had stampeded, opening the door for the destruction of Horatio Gate's army. As a result, most Continental officers, including Nathanael Greene, shared George Washington's opinion that "to place any confidence upon militia is, assuredly, resting upon a broken staff."

On occasion, however, the militia performed creditably and contributed to the success of American arms. Cowpens, just two months earlier, had offered a stunning demonstration of the potential usefulness of militia units if properly handled. Unfortunately for Greene, Daniel Morgan, the architect of the dazzling success at Cowpens had been forced by ill health to leave the army.

However, Greene was not left entirely without the "Old Wagoner's" counsel. Before he set out for home, Morgan had observed the buildup of the American army. He noted that Greene had a strong nucleus of Continentals, but that militia units comprised more than half of the army. With this in mind, Morgan wrote Greene a letter in which he succinctly analyzed the militia's role in the coming battle.

If they fight, you will beat Cornwallis; if not, he will beat you, and perhaps cut your regulars to pieces, which will be losing all our hopes.

Drawing on his recent experience at Cowpens, Morgan offered Greene his suggestions as to the best way to employ his militia forces.

I am informed that among the militia will be found a number of old soldiers. [An unspecified number of discharged Continentals were serving in the Virginia militia, as were some supernumerary Continental officers. T.B.] I think it would be advisable to select them from among the militia and put them in the ranks with the regulars; select the rifle-men also, and fight them on the flanks, under enterprising officers who are acquainted with that kind of fighting; and put the militia in the centre, with some picked troops in the rear, with orders to shoot down the first man that runs. If anything will succeed, a disposition of this kind will.

Greene noted Morgan's suggestions, but did not slavishly conform to them; rather he seemed to draw more direct inspiration from the example Morgan had set at Cowpens. In that earlier engagement, Morgan divided his army into two lines, the militia in front, the Continentals about 150 yards to their rear. Knowing that the militia line would probably break, Morgan gave these men a limited, attainable objective: Fire two rounds, then fall back, leaving the Continentals to finish off the redcoats. This plan worked far better than Morgan could have dared hope. As instructed, the militia fired their two rounds and retired. A mis-understanding of orders led the Continentals to retreat as well. As the regulars retired, they held their formation, and, on command, turned and fired a murderous volley directly into the faces of the astonished redcoats. The British panicked and were swept from the field.

Greene elected to employ a similar defense in depth at Guilford Courthouse. However, the area's terrain dictated that his army be divided into three lines and that the spaces between these positions be greater than those Morgan specified at Cowpens.

The best contemporary description of the area around Guilford Courthouse appeared in the British *Annual Register for 1781*.

The country in general presented a wilderness, covered with tall woods, which were rendered intricate by shrubs and thick underbrush; but which was interspersed here and there, by a few scattered plantations and cleared fields.

The area just west of the courthouse building particularly caught Greene's eye. This section, about a mile long, was bisected on an east-west line by New Garden Road, and was bounded in the west by Little Horsepen Creek and by Hunting Creek in the east.

The land between these streams was marked by a series of hills and gullies, and like the region in general was thickly wooded. This forest cover was occasionally broken by farm fields and old fields grown up in broom sedge with a scattering of scrub pines.

Greene believed he could make effective use of this tapestry of woodlands and clearings. The trees would break up the linear battle formations of the British, thereby reducing their effectiveness, and would also hamper Cornwallis's use of cavalry and artillery. Especially important for the unsteady American militia, the heavy timber would at times allow them to fire at the enemy from concealed positions. The redcoats, then, would be exposed to murderous volleys of musket and rifle fire as they traversed the occasional open fields in their path.

Keeping the advantages of this terrain and the example of Daniel Morgan in mind, Greene decided to divide his army into three lines. His least experienced and most unreliable troops, the North Carolina militia, would form the heart of the first line. Numbering more than 1,000 men, the North Carolinians were grouped into brigades. Brig. Gen. Thomas Eaton's brigade, composed of men from Halifax and Warren counties, formed the right wing of this line, their left flank touching New Garden Road. Running off from the left side of the road was Brig. Gen. John Butler's brigade of Orange, Guilford, and Granville county men. The Carolinians were posted behind a rail fence, facing west toward cleared fields made muddy by recent winter rains. The ends of this line extended into the woods on both sides, and were inclined slightly forward to permit a raking fire to be concentrated on the advancing redcoats.

As Morgan had suggested, the flanks were held by strong parties of riflemen, with Continental infantry and dragoons thrown in for good measure. The right flank was secured by Lt. Col. William Washington with his 100 dragoons of the 1st and 3rd Virginia regiments, as well as by Capt. Robert Kirkwood's detachment of about 40 Delaware Continentals and 200 riflemen led by Col. Charles Lynch. When he met the main army at midmorning, "Light Horse Harry" Lee took up a position on the left of the first line with his 75 cavalrymen and 80 light infantrymen, who were joined by Major Reed's detachment of mounted militia and Col. William Campbell's 250 riflemen. The center of this position was anchored by Capt. Anthony Singleton's two six-pounder cannons, which were placed in New Garden Road slightly ahead of the militia line. All in all, this was a strong position; as Lee reflected, the troops here were "most advantageously posted."

Roughly 300 yards east of the first line, in a thickly wooded zone, Greene posted two brigades of Virginia militia, about 1,200 men. Brig. Gen. Robert Lawson's troops took stations among the trees north of New Garden Road, and Brig. Gen. Edward Stevens arrayed his brigade south of that highway. Although these units were composed largely of raw recruits, a number of discharged Continental veterans were to be found scattered throughout the ranks. Some of these men had returned as draftees, while others were hired as substitutes. Together they provided a nucleus of old soldiers whose steadiness might bolster their inexperienced comrades in the coming battle.

General Stevens was determined that his men should acquit themselves honorably at Guilford Courthouse. At Camden, Stevens had commanded a detachment of Virginia militia that ran in the face of a British bayonet charge. This proud officer was clearly mortified when he concluded that the disaster at Camden had been "brought on by ye damned, rascally behavior of ye militia." To prevent a similar episode of "rascally behavior," Stevens followed the suggestion of Daniel Morgan and placed a number of riflemen twenty paces behind his lines with orders to "shoot the first man that might run . . . ."

Greene drew up his 1,400 Continentals on the western face of a hillside, a bit more than 500 yards east of the second line. These men, the cream of Greene's army, would be the last and most formidable hurdle for Lord Cornwallis's troops to clear at Guilford. As they pushed through the Virginia militia positions, the redcoats would have to pass through several hundred yards of brush and timber before they descended into a great natural amphitheater, a bowl formed by the converging downward slopes of three ridges. Local farmers had some years earlier cleared this gully (running about 1,000 yards north to south, and 250 yards east to west) to plant corn. More recently, this land had lain fallow, and broom sedge and a scattering of scrub pines had supplanted the farmers' rows of corn. Looking across the waving khaki-colored grass, the weary "lobster backs" would see the blue-coated line, the heart of Greene's army, arrayed with their backs to the forest on the hillside opposite them.

Greene elected to deploy his men in a double front formation in the fringe of wood across the brow of the hill so the Continentals could cover all the approaches to their position from across the cleared ground. The left of their line, held by Col. Benjamin Ford's 2nd Maryland Regiment, touched New Garden Road, which bisected the field. On their right was the 1st Maryland Regiment commanded by Col. John Gunby, ably seconded by Lt. Col. John Eager Howard. The right arm of the wedge was held by the Virginia regiments of Lt. Col. Samuel Hawes and Col. John Green. The center of the line, between the 1st Maryland and Hawes's regiment, was buttressed by two six-pounders directed by Lt. Ebenezer Finley. After the first line's collapse, Captain Singleton's guns were to be pulled back to a position on New Garden Road, on the left of the 2nd Maryland.

Greene's hopes for success in the coming battle rested largely on the shoulders of these 1,400 regulars. The veteran Continentals of 1781 were as reliable as their militia counterparts were unreliable. With regular army training and discipline, and the priceless benefits of battlefield experience, these veterans could fight on equal terms with even the most thoroughly seasoned redcoats.

Yet, Greene's Continentals were of uneven quality. The 2nd Maryland was essentially a new regiment, composed of recruits who had joined the army since the close of the 1780 campaign. Similarly, the Virginia regiments had been raised to replace units that had been captured at Charleston. Only the 1st Maryland was composed of solid, battle-tested veterans. In fact, the 1st was actually a hybrid unit. Her ranks were filled with the survivors of a number of Maryland regiments that had been mauled in the disastrous campaign of 1780. They had learned quickly to fight as a unit, however.

The large number of inexperienced men in the Continental regiments was probably a matter of some concern for the American commander. Nonetheless, Greene hoped that the presence of the old soldiers of the 1st Maryland would steady the recruits. The general also relied on the skill and courage of his officers, all of whom Colonel Lee lauded as being "experienced and approved."

Prudence dictated one last precaution. The army's baggage and stores were sent off to the Speedwell Ironworks on Troublesome Creek, 18 miles northeast of Guilford Courthouse. The American army had camped there occasionally in the three weeks prior to March 15, and Greene decided his army would rally there if the battle went against him.

The troop dispositions made, Greene rode over the field inspecting his lines. Aware that the North Carolina militia would be the first to feel the force of the British attack, he took special pains to encourage these men. Although Greene was no spellbinding orator, he tried to inspire the Carolinians by reminding them that they were fighting not only for liberty and independence, but also to protect their homes and families from invasion. His instructions to the militiamen, like those of Morgan at Cowpens, were pointedly simple: Fire two solid volleys at the advancing British, then fall back with their commander's blessings.

Greene realized that without bayonets, the militia would be helpless in hand-to-hand combat with the redcoats. Since they probably would break ranks, with or without orders, he decided to set a limited objective that the militiamen could realistically be expected to meet. If they achieved Greene's objective they would contribute materially to the American success, for when fired in volleys even the militiamen's motley assortment of 1,000 muskets, rifles, and fowling pieces would be devastatingly effective.

To forestall a stampede when the first line gave way, the Virginians in the second line were ordered to open their ranks and let the Carolinians pass through. The regulars on the flanks of the first line were directed to fall back and take up similar positions on the far right and left of the Virginia militia line.

The stage was now set. Having done his best to inspire and prepare the men on the first line, General Greene made his way back to the rear of the Continental position on the third line, where he would remain during the battle.

WOODS

KIRKWOOD'S DELAWARE
COMPANY

LYNCH'S RIFLE
REGIMENT

WASHINGTON'S
CAVALRY

LAWSON'S BRIGADE

AMERICAN SECOND LINE

WOODS

33RD FOOT
REGIMENT

WEBSTER

EATON'S BRIGADE

NORTH

AMERICAN FIRST LINE

VIRGINIA MILITIA

SENTINEL LINE

FENCED
FIELDS

23RD FOOT
REGIMENT

AMERICAN
ARTILLERY

CANNON

STEVENS'S BRIGADE

ROYAL
ARTILLERY

CANNON

CAROLINA

YAGERS

GRENADIER'S
GUARDS

GUARDS
LIGHT INFANTRY

PREVIOUSLY   PLANTED

BUTLER'S BRIGADE

TARLETON'S
DRAGOONS

HOSKINS
HOUSE

IN   CORN

MILITIA

TO   NEW GARDEN
MEETING HOUSE

2ND BATTALION
GUARDS

71ST HIGHLANDERS
REGIMENT

LESLIE

NORTON

1ST BATTALION
GUARDS

DUBUY

BOSE REGIMENT

CAMPBELL'S
RIFLE REGIMENT

LEE'S LEGION
CAVALRY

LEE'S LEGION
LIGHT INFANTRY

WOODS

*The first line gives way. National Park Service troop movement
plan. Scale: 1" = 1,000'*

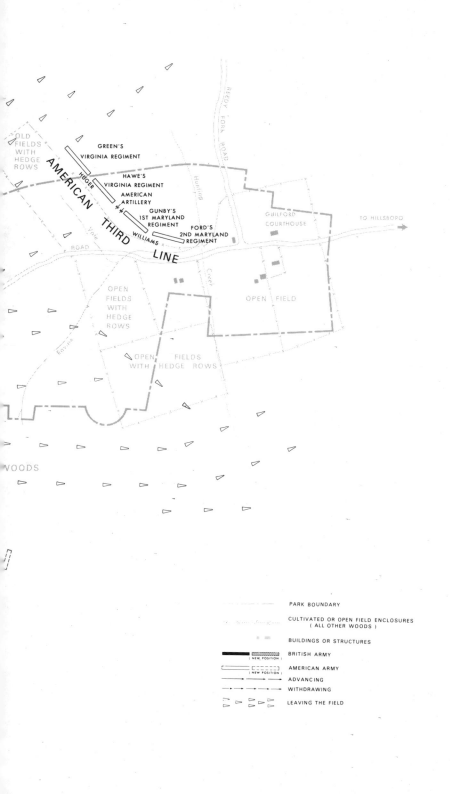

OLD
FIELDS
WITH
HEDGE
ROWS

GREEN'S
VIRGINIA REGIMENT

AMERICAN THIRD LINE

HUGER

HAWE'S
VIRGINIA REGIMENT

AMERICAN
ARTILLERY

GUNBY'S
1ST MARYLAND
REGIMENT

WILLIAMS

FORD'S
2ND MARYLAND
REGIMENT

REEDY FORK ROAD

Hunting

GUILFORD
COURTHOUSE

TO HILLSBORO

Vote

ROAD

Creek

Ravine

OPEN
FIELDS
WITH
HEDGE
ROWS

OPEN FIELD

OPEN FIELDS
WITH HEDGE ROWS

WOODS

PARK BOUNDARY

CULTIVATED OR OPEN FIELD ENCLOSURES
(ALL OTHER WOODS)

BUILDINGS OR STRUCTURES

BRITISH ARMY
(NEW POSITION)

AMERICAN ARMY
(NEW POSITION)

ADVANCING

WITHDRAWING

LEAVING THE FIELD

The First Line: Resting
Upon a Broken Staff

THE MEN in the ranks awaited the approach of the enemy with nervous expectation. One militia officer, Maj. Richard Harrison of Granville County, North Carolina, had more on his mind than just the coming battle, for his wife Nancy was about to give birth. He used this waiting time to write her an anguished note.

It is scarcely possible to paint the agitations of my mind, struggling with two of the greatest events that are in nature at the same time—the fate of my Nancy and my Country. O, my God, I trust them for the best!

Sensing the growing uneasiness among the militiamen, fiery "Light Horse Harry" Lee, now returned from the morning's fighting along New Garden Road, rode along the first line, calling on the men to stand firm and not be afraid of the British, for "he had whipped them three times that morning and could do it again."

The waiting ended around noon as the head of the British column moved down New Garden Road toward Little Horsepen Creek, about 800 yards down the hill from the first line. As the redcoats began to ford the stream, Captain Singleton opened fire with his six-pounders. Lord Cornwallis, present and directing the movements of his army, halted his column and ordered Lieutenant MacLeod to bring up two three-pounders and return the enemy's fire. While the big guns blazed away, Cornwallis crossed all of his troops over Little Horsepen, and, using the woods on both sides of the road for cover, deployed them for battle.

The artillery duel lasted about 30 minutes. Aside from filling the air with sulfurous smoke, the cannon fire produced few tangible results, with only a handful of men and artillery horses on each side killed or wounded. But, the already apprehensive militiamen were probably further unnerved by the thunderous hammering of the guns and the wild screeching of cannon balls as they caromed through the treetops around them.

Lord Cornwallis was relatively ignorant of the terrain around Guilford Courthouse. The British army had passed through the area while pursuing the rebels to the Dan, but Cornwallis had been too preoccupied then to carefully note the lay of the land. The earl was likewise ignorant of the enemy's troop dispositions, the thick forest concealing all but the center of the American first line from view. Even though he was unable to obtain reliable information from local citizens, Cornwallis apparently made only cursory efforts to reconnoiter the area and based his battle plans only on what he saw before him. He explained his conclusions in his report of the battle.

The woods on our right and left were reported to be impracticable for cannon; but as that on our right appeared the most open, I resolved to attack the left wing of the enemy.

This decision made, Cornwallis deployed his troops for battle. On his right, south of New Garden Road, he placed Lt. Col. Duncan McPherson's 71st Regiment of Foot. The 71st was a regiment of Scotch Highlanders, easily recognizable by the traditional Highland bonnets they wore. On their right were the blue-coated Hessians of Lt. Col. Johann Christian DuBuy's Regiment von Bose. Totaling 565 officers and men, this wing was under the direction of Maj. Gen. Alexander Leslie, a brave and experienced officer who ultimately would succeed Cornwallis as British commander in the southern theater. In reserve, Leslie had at his disposal about 200 men of Lieutenant Colonel Norton's 1st Battalion of Guards.

North of the road, Lt. Col. James Webster led 472 men of the 23rd and 33rd Regiments of Foot. Lt. Col. Nesbitt Balfour's 23rd, also known as the Royal Welch Fusiliers, was a veteran regiment whose motto, *Ich dien*, meant, "I serve."

Cornwallis's old outfit, the 33rd, was one of the finest, most experienced units in the British army. Its commander, Lieutenant Colonel Webster, had brought his regiment to America in early 1776, and they had served brilliantly in both the northern and southern campaigns. Webster was described in glowing terms by Sir Henry Clinton as "an officer of great experience, and on whom I reposed the most explicit confidence." Likewise, Cornwallis both admired and was personally close to the younger regimental commander. When Webster later died of wounds received at Guilford Courthouse, Cornwallis lamented, "I have lost my scabbard."

Webster's auxiliaries consisted of 84 jaegers and about 50 light infantrymen of the Guards. Also in reserve, with instructions to support Webster, was Brig. Gen. Charles O'Hara with 250 men of the 2nd Battalion of Guards. O'Hara was one of Cornwallis's most colorful subordinates. An Irishman, he had entered the army as a teenager, as had most of the career officers in the king's service. Before the American Revolution he had been stationed in Germany, Portugal, and on the west coast of Africa, where he commanded a regiment of convicts who had been pardoned in return for a lifetime of military service in Senegal. Clinton described the roguish O'Hara as "a great, nay plausible, talker." O'Hara headed the largest unit in Cornwallis's army, the Brigade of Guards. In the coming battle, O'Hara would personally direct the 2nd Battalion and the grenadier company of Guards.

As originally constituted, the British line of battle measured about 1,000 yards. This was 200 to 300 yards shorter than the American front. However, when the reserves moved up, the line expanded to slightly overlap the rebel flanks. This extension required all of Cornwallis's troops, with the exception of the Royal Artillery detachment and Tarleton's cavalry, which followed the infantry along New Garden Road.

Although there is some disagreement as to the precise time, the British lines apparently stepped forward at about 1 P.M. For the uninitiated North Carolinians, it must have been an imposing spectacle. To the roll of their drums, the redcoats marched ahead, shoulder-to-shoulder, with polished musket barrels and bayonets flashing in the afternoon sun. Their faded regimental banners snapping in the March wind, the British slogged through the mire of wet corn fields with—in the words of one of their admiring officers—"steady and guarded, but firm and determined resolution."

The redcoats had to cross about 400 yards of rising, open ground to reach the American position. As they pressed closer, they saw, as Sgt. Roger Lamb of the Royal Welch Fusiliers recalled, that the militiamen "had their arms presented, and resting on a rail fence . . . . They were taking aim with the nicest precision." Lamb noted that this forbidding sight broke the redcoats' fabled aplomb, causing them to pause momentarily before the fence. This temporary irresolution was shattered by Colonel Webster, who galloped forward shouting, "Come on, my brave Fusiliers!" The Fusiliers, Highlanders, Hessians, and Guards all responded, driving on to within 140 yards of the fence, where the Americans opened fire. Hundreds of flintlocks flashed and roared, and clouds of pungent black powder smoke rolled down toward the advancing redcoats. On the British right, Capt. Dugald Stuart of the 71st remembered that instant well, for "One half of the Highlanders dropped on that spot . . . ." Behind the fence, militiaman William Montgomery gazed through the haze of gunsmoke and saw that this volley had torn the British lines so they resembled "the scattering stalks in a wheat field, when the harvest man has passed over it with his cradle."

In spite of their losses, the redcoats closed ranks, stepped over their dead, and marched on "in profound silence, with bayonets fixed and muskets sloped." At about 50 yards distance, the British halted, and fired a volley into the Americans. Then, with wild shouts and cheers, they raced toward the fence. This was too much for many of the militiamen to bear. As British commissary Charles Stedman commented wryly, "The enemy did not wait the shock, but retreated behind the second line." The center of the first line crumbled as frightened men threw away arms and equipment, and disregarding the pleas of their officers fled before the incoming tide of bayonets. "Light Horse Harry" Lee, incensed by the militiamen's flight, threatened to turn his cavalry on the fugitives, but to no avail.

Although critical of the North Carolina militia as a whole, Lee spoke approvingly of a group of Carolinians who attached themselves to Campbell's riflemen and the legion, and fought on after the remainder of the first line collapsed.

A few other militiamen held on along the fence and struggled against the redcoats until driven back by the enemy's overwhelming numbers. Among these diehards was Capt. Arthur Forbis of Guilford County, North Carolina. Forbis, who commanded a company of 25 men posted on the American left, proved his prowess as a marksman early in the action when he picked off a conspicuous British officer as the enemy stormed up the hillside. In the struggle along the fence, Forbis was mortally wounded, suffering gunshot wounds in his neck and leg.

While the center of the first line was breaking, the riflemen and Continentals on the flanks held firm, raking the British lines with accurate gunfire. To counter these twin threats on their flanks, the British extended their lines on the right and left, pushing up all of their infantry reserves to fill the gaps in their lines. On the British right, the 1st Battalion of Guards moved up to support the Regiment von Bose against Campbell's riflemen and Lee's legionnaires. Likewise, on the left, where Lynch's riflemen and Capt. Robert Kirkwood's Delaware Continentals blazed away at the exposed flank of the British 33rd Regiment, Colonel Webster changed his front to the left, and with the support of the jaegers and light infantry of the Guards, drove the Americans back. The gap between Webster's right was filled by the grenadiers and 2nd Battalion of Guards under O'Hara.

Overpowered, Lynch and Kirkwood, covered by Washington's cavalry, retired to the right flank on the second line, fighting there for a time before retreating to the third line. On the American left, Lee and Campbell, with some of the militia, fell back, closely followed by Norton's 1st Battalion of Guards and the Regiment von Bose.

As Lee's party retired, it veered off to the southeast, bypassing its assigned position on the left of the second line. Drawing the Guards and Hessians in their wake, these antagonists became embroiled in their own private battle, isolated from the second and third line fighting. Although detached from the main struggle, this sideshow was of some importance in determining the eventual outcome of the Battle of Guilford Courthouse, for it deprived both commanders of troops that could have been put to better use on other parts of the field.

Certainly Cornwallis's outnumbered redcoats soon would need every man available to support them. They had routed the first line, but had suffered casualties in the process. Already their reserves—save the cavalry and artillery—had been committed to the struggle. Ahead lay heavy forest, concealing a much more combative Virginia militia line. For the British, the real battle was just beginning.

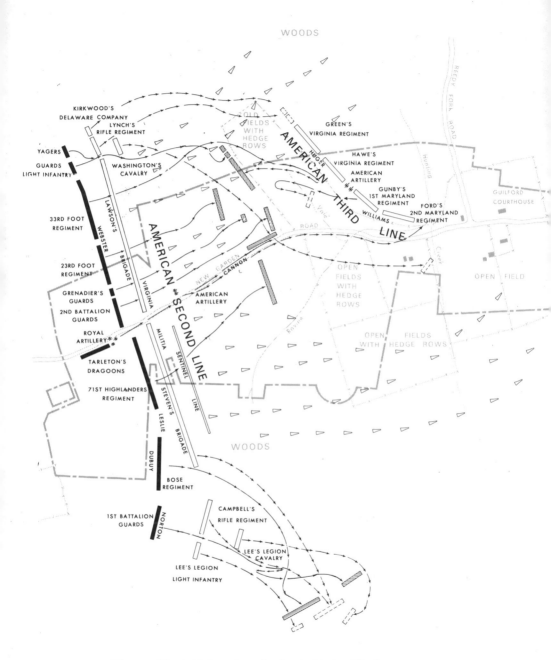

WOODS

KIRKWOOD'S
DELAWARE COMPANY
LYNCH'S
RIFLE REGIMENT

YAGERS

GUARDS
LIGHT INFANTRY

WASHINGTON'S
CAVALRY

OLD
FIELDS
WITH
HEDGE
ROWS

GREEN'S
VIRGINIA REGIMENT

AMERICAN THIRD LINE

HUGER

HAWE'S
VIRGINIA REGIMENT
AMERICAN
ARTILLERY

GUNBY'S
1ST MARYLAND
REGIMENT

WILLIAMS

FORD'S
2ND MARYLAND
REGIMENT

GUILFORD
COURTHOUSE

REEDY FORK ROAD

33RD FOOT
REGIMENT

LAWSON'S

WEBSTER

BRIGADE

VIRGINIA

AMERICAN SECOND LINE

NEW GARDEN

CANNON

ROAD

Nole

Hunting

Creek

OPEN
FIELDS
WITH
HEDGE
ROWS

OPEN FIELD

23RD FOOT
REGIMENT

GRENADIER'S
GUARDS

2ND BATTALION
GUARDS

ROYAL
ARTILLERY **

TARLETON'S
DRAGOONS

71ST HIGHLANDERS
REGIMENT

MILITIA

STEVEN'S BRIGADE

SENTINEL LINE

AMERICAN
ARTILLERY

Rovier

OPEN FIELDS
WITH HEDGE ROWS

LESLIE

DUBUY

BOSE
REGIMENT

1ST BATTALION
GUARDS

NORTON

CAMPBELL'S
RIFLE REGIMENT

LEE'S LEGION
CAVALRY

LEE'S LEGION
LIGHT INFANTRY

WOODS

*The second line holds for a time, then breaks. National Park
Service troop movement plan. Scale: 1" = 1,000'*

The Second Line: "A Fierce and Fatal Fire"

As the redcoats drove through the first line, the forest that engulfed them accomplished what the North Carolina militia could not: It broke the British battle formations into fragments. Used to fighting shoulder-to-shoulder in a sort of hedgehog of bayonets, the British now found their ranks shattered as men scrambled through a maze of heavy forest and thick undergrowth along zigzag paths. Thus, the fighting on the second line often broke down into a series of small unit actions in which handfuls of British infantrymen struggled to root out pockets of concealed American riflemen. Commissary Stedman aptly characterized the second line struggle as "an action of almost infinite diversity."

Confusion reigned from end to end along the British front.

Nowhere was this chaos greater than on Gen. Alexander Leslie's right wing, where the 71st Highlanders faced Edward Stevens's Virginians virtually alone. The Highlanders had suffered heavy casualties on the first line and these losses were compounded by the irregular but "fierce and fatal" gunfire directed at them by the Virginia militia.

On the periphery, the Guards and the von Bose regiment were even more heavily engaged. In the words of Charles Stedman, "this part of the British line was at times warmly engaged in front, flank, and rear, with some of the enemy that had been routed in the first attack, and with part of the extremity of their left wing, which, by the closeness of the woods, had been passed unseen."

Fighting on the extreme left of the second American line was a twenty-two year old Virginian named Samuel Houston. As the Guards moved off to the southeast, Houston and a number of his comrades left their places in the line to pounce on the unsuspecting lobster backs. Houston wrote: "We fired on their flank, and that brought down many of them . . . . We pursued them about forty poles to the top of a hill, where they stood, and we retreated from them back to where we formed."

Although the Guards survived this ambush, they soon encountered another irregular rebel line atop a steep hill. As the redcoats struggled up the slope, the Americans would pop over the summit, fire their weapons, and retire behind the back side of the hill to reload. This tactic exacted a heavy toll of British officers and men in the ascent. Nonetheless, the Guards finally succeeded in driving off the enemy with their bayonets.

No sooner had they done so, however, than they encountered another body of rebel troops which opened fire on them. Winded by their exertions, and with many of their officers already down, the guardsmen temporarily forgot their vaunted discipline and ran away. They were saved from total destruction by the arrival of the Regiment von Bose, which advanced to cover the Guards while their remaining officers rallied the dispirited men. Indicative of the confusion on the second line, the Americans at first mistook the Hessians to be rebels, probably because they wore blue coats similar to those of the Continentals. This misapprehension was corrected when the Americans cried out the catchword "Liberty!" and were answered by a hail of musket fire.

Fighting on the British right continued in the same vein long after the second line gave way. As Charles Stedman reported, each time the Guards and Hessians defeated an enemy detachment in their front "they found it necessary to return and attack another body of them that had appeared in their rear, [and] in this manner they were obliged to traverse the same ground in various directions."

The British made better progress on their left where the 33rd Regiment and the 2nd Battalion of Guards pushed steadily through Lawson's Virginians. In this area, militia officers like St. George Tucker struggled manfully to hold off the advancing redcoats While moving with his own and another American regiment to attack the flank of an advancing British unit, Tucker discovered that the enemy had gotten "in our rear." Tucker disgustedly reported that this development so completely unnerved the militia that they "instantly broke off without firing a single gun and dispersed like a flock of sheep frightened by dogs."

With "infinite labor," Tucker and another officer managed to collect about 70 of the fugitives and take up "an irregular kind of skirmishing with the British, and were once successful enough to drive a party for a very small distance." Despite such momentary setbacks, the 33rd Regiment and the 2nd Battalion of Guards pressed resolutely forward.

Between the 33rd and the Guards, the 23rd Regiment—the Royal Welch Fusiliers—became bogged down. One of the officers of the 23rd, Sir Thomas Saumarez, described a struggle to dislodge a detachment of Virginians whom the redcoats discovered "formed behind brushwood."

Not being able to attack in front, the Fusiliers were obliged to take the ground to their left to get clear of the brushwood. They then attacked the enemy with the bayonet in so cool and deliberate a manner as to throw the Americans into the greatest confusion and disperse them.

Although successful in this skirmish, the 23rd still lagged behind the 33rd Regiment and the 2nd Guards.

While the 23rd groped forward, one of its noncommissioned officers, Sgt. Roger Lamb, became separated from his unit. Lamb stopped in the area passed over by the 2nd Battalion of Guards when he unexpectedly encountered several parties of Virginians. While filling his cartridge box with ammunition taken from a dead guardsman, Lamb observed another solitary Englishman riding toward the concealed Americans.

This was none other than the commander of the British army, Lord Charles Cornwallis. Early in the second line fighting, Cornwallis had become concerned by the slow progress on the British right, and had ridden over to personally encourage Leslie's troops. While on the right, the general's horse had been shot from under him, and he had remounted himself on a cavalryman's steed. Lamb left a graphic description of Cornwallis's almost comic appearance.

His lordship was mounted on a dragoon's horse; the saddlebags were under the creature's belly, which much retarded his progress; owing to the vast quantity of underwood that was spread over the ground; his lordship was evidently unconscious of his danger.

Lamb at once seized the horse's bridle and led Cornwallis to the relative safety afforded by the 23rd Regiment.

On the American right flank, where the Delaware company, Lynch's riflemen, and Washington's cavalry had taken up a new position following the collapse of the first line, the jaegers' and Guards' light infantry were heavily engaged. Sgt. William Seymour of Delaware noted with pride that "our riflemen and musketry behaved with great bravery, killing and wounding great numbers of the enemy." Nonetheless, this doughty little band was pushed aside by superior British numbers.

Likewise, Webster's 33rd and the 2nd Battalion of Guards north of New Garden Road broke through Lawson's line. The destruction of the second line was completed when the 23rd and 71st regiments finally drove off the Americans on their fronts.

Like their neighbors in the first line, most of the Virginians scattered away from the fighting. However, Col. James Martin of North Carolina had been ordered by General Greene to rally the militia at the courthouse, and this officer succeeded in rounding up about 500 of the fugitives from the first and second lines. Although Martin was unable to throw these men back into the fighting before General Greene issued his retreat order, these militiamen enjoyed a grandstand view of the third line action from the courthouse.

Among the Virginians who congregated at the courthouse was Edward Stevens. General Stevens was in great pain, having suffered a severe musket-ball wound in his thigh. As the army surgeons dressed his injured leg, however, Stevens reflected with satisfaction on the performance of his militia. He later wrote, "The brigade behaved with the greatest bravery, and stood till I ordered their retreat."

Although not all of the men on the second line were deserving of such praise, most of the Virginia militia had behaved admirably. They had taken on the bulk of Cornwallis's army and, while not defeating the enemy, had dealt them a heavy blow. Making good use of the terrain about them, the militia engaged the British in a taxing series of running fire fights, which left the floor of the forest strewn with dead and wounded redcoats. When the British reached the third line they were physically exhausted, their forces scattered, and significantly depleted. Five hundred of their comrades of the 1st Guards and the von Bose regiment were still somewhere to the south, struggling furiously with Lee's infantry and militiamen—too far off to come to their aid. Ahead lay the sternest test of an already bloody day: Nathanael Greene's 1,400 Continentals.

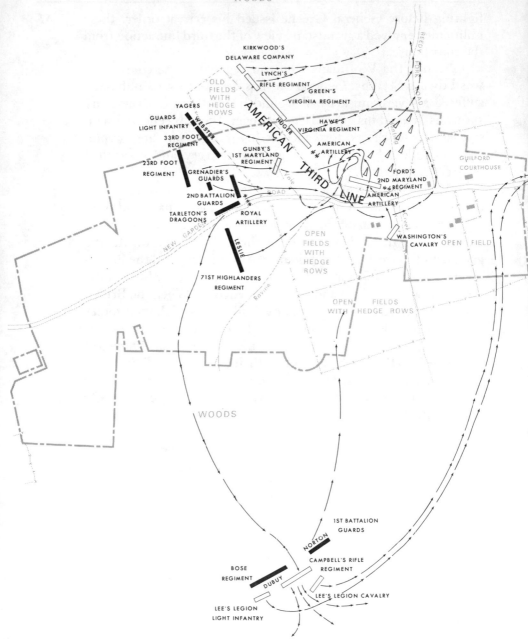

WOODS

KIRKWOOD'S
DELAWARE COMPANY

LYNCH'S
RIFLE REGIMENT

GREEN'S
VIRGINIA REGIMENT

OLD
FIELDS
WITH
HEDGE
ROWS

YAGERS

GUARDS
LIGHT INFANTRY

33RD FOOT
REGIMENT

23RD FOOT
REGIMENT

GRENADIER'S
GUARDS

2ND BATTALION
GUARDS

TARLETON'S
DRAGOONS

ROYAL
ARTILLERY

71ST HIGHLANDERS
REGIMENT

WEBSTER

HUGER

AMERICAN THIRD LINE

HAWE'S
VIRGINIA REGIMENT

AMERICAN
ARTILLERY

GUNBY'S
1ST MARYLAND
REGIMENT

FORD'S
2ND MARYLAND
REGIMENT

AMERICAN
ARTILLERY

LESLIE

GUILFORD
COURTHOUSE

REEDY FORK ROAD

WASHINGTON'S
CAVALRY

OPEN
FIELDS
WITH
HEDGE
ROWS

OPEN FIELD

NEW GARDEN ROAD

OPEN FIELDS
WITH HEDGE ROWS

WOODS

1ST BATTALION
GUARDS

NORTON

BOSE
REGIMENT

DUBUY

CAMPBELL'S RIFLE
REGIMENT

LEE'S LEGION CAVALRY

LEE'S LEGION
LIGHT INFANTRY

*Decision on the third line and retreat. National Park Service
troop movement plan. Scale: 1" = 1,000'*

"We Were Immediately Engaged
with the Guards"

Standing quietly in their ranks on the hillside west of the courthouse, Greene's Continentals waited, anxiously scanning the open ground before them. The wilderness completely hid the final scenes of the furious struggle from the regulars' view, although they were separated from the second line by only a few hundred yards. They could only listen as the roar of gunfire edged closer to them.

Finally, knots of Virginia militiamen appeared, scampering across the ravine and into the safety of the forest beyond—a sure sign that the second line had begun to give way. As this trickle of fugitives grew into a steady stream, a few organized bodies of troops appeared and took up positions. The first of these were

Kirkwood's Delawares and Lynch's riflemen, winded by their struggles on the first and second lines but ready to "push bayonets" with the redcoats one more time. These pugnacious veterans fell in on the far right near Col. John Green's Virginians. Behind them came William Washington's dragoons, cantering along the Continentals' front to a vantage point atop the steep hill that commanded the field from the south.

Shortly, men in different colored uniforms violated the northern end of the clearing. Soldiers in red coats and green coats—the 23rd Regiment, the light infantry of the Guards, and the jaegers—broke out of the tree line and plunged into the ravine. Without waiting for the other British units to come to his support, the gallant Lt. Col. James Webster led his men to attack the American lines—with what Colonel Lee called "more ardour than prudence." Storming up the western slope toward the Continentals, the jaegers and light infantry on Webster's left closed with Hawes's Virginia regiment. On his right, the 33rd was on a collision course with the 1st Maryland. The Americans allowed the British to sweep on unopposed, until at very close range—perhaps as little as 20 yards—the Continental officers shouted the command: "Fire!" A crashing volley swept down the hillside, toppling many of the redcoats, including Colonel Webster, whose knee was shattered by a musket ball. It it likely that only part of the Continental line had been visible to Webster across the broom sedge and scrub pines. Realizing now that they were seriously outnumbered, he and his redcoats retraced their steps across the cleared ground to the cover of the forest.

As the action on the American right died out, more British troops began to emerge from the trees. The first of these units, the 2nd Battalion of Guards, appeared just north of New Garden Road. The 2nd Guards had entered the battle under the personal direction of the colorful Brig. Gen. Charles O'Hara. However, in breaching the two militia lines, O'Hara had suffered two dangerous wounds, and command of the Guards had passed to Lt. Col. James Stuart. Stuart led the Guards, "glowing with impatience to signalize themselves," toward the only part of the American line clearly visible to them: Ford's 2nd Maryland Regiment and Captain Singleton's two six-pounders which were located in the roadway.

Having observed with satisfaction the performance of the 1st Maryland against the 33rd, Col. Otho Williams, commander of the Maryland brigade, "hastened toward the second, expecting a similar display." He was appalled, however, when the 2nd Maryland fired one weak volley at the oncoming Guards and then bolted. Panicking, the Marylanders broke ranks and fled into the woods in their rear. The Guards seized Singleton's cannons and exuberantly pursued Colonel Ford's rabble into the forest.

The Guards had opened a serious—perhaps fatal—breech in the American position. Having turned the rebels' left flank, the Guards could now pounce on the rear, or even encircle the remainder, of the Continental line. Should the 33rd or any of the other British units then arriving on the field press the attack from the front, the Americans would be crushed between the jaws of a red-coated vise. Seeing this, Greene concluded that it would be "most advisable to order a retreat." The general immediately acted on his decision, directing Col. John Green to pull his Virginia regiment out of the line to cover the army's withdrawal. However, the roar of gunfire and dense smoke made battlefield communications uncertain. The fighting was by now out of Greene's hands and was being directed by individual unit commanders, some of whom were not yet ready to admit defeat.

As the Guards rolled over the 2nd Maryland, Gunby's 1st Maryland, on the redcoats' immediate left, was concealed from view by a small copse. Informed by a deputy adjutant general that the Guards were pushing into the woods in his rear, Lt. Col. John Eager Howard, second in command of the 1st Maryland, wrote:

I rode to Colonel Gunby and gave him the information. He did not hesitate to order the regiment to face about, and we were immediately engaged with the guards. Our men gave them some well directed fires, and we then advanced and continued firing.

Nathaniel Slade, a North Carolina militiaman who watched from the courthouse, attested to the ferocity of this attack.

This conflict between the brigade of guards and the first regiment of Marylanders was most terrific, for they fired at the same instant, and they appeared so near that the blazes from the muzzles of their guns seemed to meet.

As the Marylanders turned on the Guards, Colonel Gunby's horse was shot and fell, pinning its rider. The command of the regiment then passed into the capable hands of Lieutenant Colonel Howard. John Eager Howard was one of the most distinguished field officers in the American army. He had fought in virtually every major battle of the war, in both the North and in the South. For his conspicuous role in the Battle of Cowpens, Congress awarded Howard a gold medal, one of only eight such rewards presented during the war. Nathanael Greene called his gallant subordinate "as good an officer as the world affords."

Howard later recalled that as he led the attack "I observed Washington's horse, and as their movements were quicker than ours, they first charged and broke the enemy." From his vantage point atop the steep hill at the southern end of the clearing, William Washington had observed the route of the 2nd Maryland. Washington's stout frame and cherubic face belied his combative nature. A cousin of commander-in-chief George Washington, William Washington had been a divinity student at the outbreak of the Revolution. He exchanged his books for a cavalry saber in early 1776, and since had distinguished himself as a bold and energetic leader of mounted troops. Seeing in the flight of the 2nd Maryland a chance to surprise and inflict severe damage upon the enemy, Washington ordered his trumpeter to sound the charge. Like a mountain avalanche, the dragoons rolled down the hillside and smashed squarely into the rear of the Guards.

Riding with Washington's cavalry was Thomas Watkins's company of dragoons from Prince Edward County, Virginia. Lt. Philemon Holcomb of Watkins's company described the charge.

Leaping a ravine, the swords of the horsemen were upon the enemy, who were rejoicing in victory and safety; and before they suspected danger, multitudes lay dead.

The momentum of Washington's charge carried his men all the way through the tangled British ranks. They then turned and rode through again, sabering the redcoats as they went. Particularly conspicuous among the troopers was Peter Francisco, a young Virginian of awesome size for his time. Standing six and one-half feet tall and weighing at least 260 pounds, Francisco

Lt. Col. John Eager Howard (1752-1827). This late nineteenth-century engraving probably depends on a portrait by Charles Willson Peale.

wielded an equally awesome cavalry saber that measured five feet in length. With this monstrous weapon, the "Virginia giant" cut down eleven of the guardsmen before being felled himself by a frightful bayonet wound in the leg.

Reeling from the shock of the cavalry attack, the Guards were assaulted on their flank by the 1st Maryland. Colonel Howard wrote:

My men followed very quickly, and we pressed through the guards, many of whom had been knocked down by the horse without being much hurt. We took some prisoners, and the whole were in our power.

In vicious hand-to-hand fighting, the 1st Maryland drove the redcoats back into the cleared ground and recovered the six-pounders so recently lost by their comrades.

The field was covered by men shooting, clubbing, and stabbing each other, but a bitter encounter between a British and an

68   American officer was particularly notable. Virtually everyone who has chronicled the Battle of Guilford Courthouse has recounted the clash between Capt. John Smith of the 1st Maryland and Col. James Stuart of the Guards. The best, most evocative, of these descriptions was written by Greene's commissary general, Col. William R. Davie.

Smith and his men were in a throng, killing the Guards and Grenadiers like so many Furies. Colonel Stewart [sic], seeing the mischief Smith was doing, made up to him through the crowd, dust, and smoke, and made a violent lunge at him with his small sword . . . . It would have run through his body but for the haste of the Colonel, and happening to set his foot on the arm of a man Smith had just cut down, his unsteady step, his violent lunge, and missing his aim brought him down to one knee on the dead man. The Guards came rushing up very strong. Smith had no alternative but to wheel around and give Stewart [sic] a back-handed blow over, or across the head, on which he fell.

Stuart's orderly sergeant next attacked Smith, but was struck down by a Marylander. Smith then killed one more guardsman before he was finally shot in the back of his head by a redcoat. The wounded American officer was carried off the field by his men. Remarkably, he recovered from his injury.

    After completing his second circuit through the Guards, William Washington caught sight of a British officer with several aides riding forward, as if to make a reconnaisance. Washington at once concluded that the redcoat must be Lord Cornwallis, and spurring his horse forward, he led a group of dragoons to capture this prize. Sensing the approaching danger, however, the British officer rode back to his own lines. (Another version of this story has it that, in the chase, Washington lost the leather helmet which he wore to protect his head from saber cuts. Reining in to retrieve this vital piece of headgear, another officer took the lead of the column. When this officer was shot, his horse bolted to the rear. Seeing their leader riding away, the dragoons assumed the chase was over, and followed.)

    Washington was probably correct in assuming that this enemy officer was Cornwallis. The British general did ride forward to observe the fighting in which the Guards were embroiled;

Col. William Washington (1752-1810). Mezzotint after painting by Charles Willson Peale.

he did not like what he saw. The Guards were being mercilessly pounded between the hammer and anvil of the 1st Maryland and Washington's cavalry, and radical measures would be required to save them from total annihilation.

Riding back to his own lines, Cornwallis sought out his artillery chief, Lieutenant MacLeod, who had just reached the front with two guns. The general directed the young officer to place his three-pounders on the western slope of the ravine and fire charges of grapeshot directly into the tangle of contending American and British troops below. General O'Hara, whose wounds had prevented his personal involvement in the third line fighting, over-heard these instructions and vehemently protested that many of his guardsmen would be killed by this fire. Cornwallis refused to countermand his order.

With crisp precision, the British artillerymen rammed the grapeshot charges into their three-pounders. When the gunners touched off their pieces, the little guns lurched backward and scores of iron balls slammed into the melee below, cutting down Continentals and redcoats alike. Harsh as this action was, it did achieve its intended purpose. The stunning scatter-gun effect of grapeshot at close range stopped the 1st Maryland and Washington's dragoons in their tracks, allowing the Guards to escape back to the British lines.

As Howard rallied his bewildered Marylanders, he saw that other British units were appearing on the field. First among these late arrivals were the 71st Regiment and the grenadiers of the Guards. Long delayed by the stubborn resistance of Stevens's Virginians and the rough terrain that they were required to traverse, these outfits moved into line on the right of the Guards. Although wounded, General O'Hara meanwhile rallied the shattered Guards with his own "spirited exertions." Likewise, Colonel Webster, forgetting his own painful injury, reformed the 33rd. The last gap in the British front was filled when the Royal Welch Fusiliers finally moved into position north of New Garden Road.

The gallant Howard realized that the pendulum of battle had swung back in favor of the British. The retreat that Greene had ordered now had become general. Aside from his doughty Marylanders and Washington's cavalry, the only organized body of American troops remaining on the field was Hawes's Virginia regiment of Huger's brigade. The Continentals were probably outnumbered two to one by the redcoats.

Howard wisely accepted the hopelessness of his situation and ordered his men to retire. Washington's dragoons followed. True veterans that they were, the Marylanders withdrew in good order, even though they came under enemy fire from an unexpected source. Howard reported that "many of the guards who were lying on the ground and who we supposed were wounded, got up and fired at us as we retired." Huger's Virginians held their position just long enough to beat off one last attack by Webster's 33rd Regiment. Of this, General Greene reported simply that "General Huger was the last that was engaged, and he gave the enemy a check."

As Huger's Continentals disappeared from his front, Cornwallis saw that victory was at last within his grasp. He at once issued orders to exploit his advantage. The 23rd and 71st regiments were directed to pursue the retreating rebels. Because most of their artillery horses had been killed, the Americans were obliged to leave their four six-pounders behind, and these prizes once more fell into the redcoats' hands. Part of Tarleton's cavalry, which reached the front during the last stages of the fighting, also was thrown into the chase. Tarleton himself was dispatched with his remaining horsemen to the far right, where "a heavy fire still continued."

The fringe battle had, by the time the third line fighting concluded, moved to a hill about a mile south of the center of the main British formation. Although the struggle there remained fierce, "Light Horse Harry" Lee detected that Colonel Norton was apparently trying to slip away with his Guards to rendezvous with Cornwallis's forces near the courthouse. Lee decided to seize this opportunity to rejoin Greene. Pushing the Hessians at their front back a short distance, Lee's cavalry, infantry, and one company of riflemen "pressed forward to join the Continentals, and to take their appropriate station on their left."

The timing of this movement proved to be unfortunate. When he arrived in the vicinity of the courthouse, Lee found that Greene had already withdrawn. Too late to take part in the third line fighting, "Light Horse Harry" led his troops around Cornwallis's right flank and followed Greene's retreating forces along a parallel road.

Lee's departure placed Campbell's riflemen in an extremely critical situation, with no cavalry to cover their own retreat. When Colonel Tarleton, acting on Cornwallis's orders, arrived on the right, Major Dubuy's Hessians were directed to "fire a volley upon the heaviest part of the militia." Tarleton's troopers then charged out of the covering haze of gunsmoke and overran the American position. Samuel Houston recalled sadly, "We were obliged to run, and many were sore chased, and some cut down."

On this rather anticlimactic note, the Battle of Guilford Courthouse ended. It was around 3:30 P.M. as Campbell's riflemen fled into the forest—some would rejoin Greene's army the following day, others would never be heard from again.

For the remainder of his life, Nathanael Greene believed that if only the North Carolina militia had held its position a bit longer, his army would have won the Battle of Guilford Courthouse. The disappointed American commander wrote Gov. Abner Nash of North Carolina: "We ought to have had victory and had your militia stood by their officers it was certain." Greene went so far in his denunciations of the Carolinians' craven behavior as to assert that "none fired more than twice, and near half not at all."

Perhaps if Greene had been present during the first stage of the fighting he would have tempered his judgment of the militia's performance. There were numerous testimonials to the North Carolinians' effective resistance by participants who had been close to the scene.

British officers such as Sir Thomas Saumarez ("The regiment marched to the attack under a most galling and destructive fire . . .") and Capt. Dugald Stuart ("We received a very deadly fire . . .") attested to the harsh receptions their regiments received from the Americans, who also had praise for their first line militia. Samuel Houston recounted that some of the Carolinians remained in position long enough to fire three rounds at the enemy before retiring. This was truly service above and beyond the call of duty, for General Greene's orders directed the militia to fire only two volleys before withdrawing. Indeed, it is difficult to fathom Greene's criticism—"none fired more than twice"—in light of these instructions.

Considering their lack of discipline, experience, and bayonets, the North Carolina militia probably performed as well as could reasonably have been expected. As Capt. Anthony Singleton, a Continental officer who observed a good deal of the first line fighting, concluded, "The militia, contrary to custom, behaved well for militia." It is difficult, therefore, to accept Greene's assessment that the cowardice of the North Carolina militia robbed the American army of its chance for victory. In fact, this harsh analysis smacks of the well-known antimilitia prejudice that Greene shared with many other Continental officers.

Greene should have known the immediate cause of the American defeat at Guilford Courthouse, for he was on the scene and personally issued the order that initiated the retreat. The American withdrawal was occasioned by the precipitate flight of the 2nd Maryland Regiment. It was the collapse of the Continentals' left flank that compromised the entire third line and led the commanding general to abandon the fight. Had the Continentals maintained the integrity of their position, they might have crushed the scattered and bleeding British units as they launched their piecemeal attacks. For that matter, the performance of the 1st Maryland and Washington's cavalry suggested that if the American commander had delayed his decision to retreat, the Continentals could have turned the tide against the redcoats. It is perhaps the supreme irony of the Battle of Guilford Courthouse that the fiercest fighting of the day took place after Greene had decided to abandon the field.

General Greene could not have foreseen this development, and even if he had it is unlikely that he would have countermanded his order. Knowing the history of the war in the South as he did, he firmly believed his own admonition to Daniel Morgan: "It is not our business to risk too much." For the time being, Greene would console himself with the knowledge that his army had fought well enough to sell Lord Cornwallis a very insignificant piece of real estate at a very high price.

"Another Such Victory . . ."

NATHANAEL GREENE'S ARMY fell back from the third line field to the Reedy Fork Road, just west of the courthouse. Turning north, the Americans tramped three miles, forded Reedy Fork Creek, then halted for several hours to collect their stragglers. In spite of some early confusion, the withdrawal had been conducted in orderly fashion. The good order of this movement, in turn, dissuaded the British from making more than a halfhearted pursuit.

St. George Tucker, who fell in near the rear of the retreating column, wrote that a troop of British dragoons attempted to ride down the fugitives, "but a party of Continentals [Greene's Virginia regiment] who were fortunately close behind us, gave him so warm a reception that he retreated with some degree of precipitation." Tucker later saw a British officer observing the Americans from a distance, but "he did not think it proper to attack us again . . . ."

After pausing along the Reedy Fork, the Americans resumed their retreat. Without definite information as to the condition of the British forces or their battle losses, Greene only could assume that the redcoats would soon follow to exploit their victory. He therefore drove his weary army on through the gathering darkness toward its old campground at the Speedwell Iron Works. As the men plodded along, a cold winter rain began to fall, adding to the general discomfort and gloom of the night.

The roads leading north were scattered with groups of men trailing in the wake of the main army. Samuel Houston was among these men. Having narrowly escaped Tarleton's dragoons after the disastrous termination of the fringe battle, Houston and a few comrades struck out to rejoin the army.

We marched for headquarters, and marched till we, about dark, came to the road we marched up from Reedy Creek to Guilford the day before, and crossing the creek we marched near four miles, and our wounded, Lusk, Allison, and in particular Jas. Mather, who was bad cut, were so sick we stopped and all being almost wearied out, we marched half a mile, and encamped, where, through the darkness and rain, and want of provisions we were in distress. Some parched a little corn. We stretched blankets to protect us from the rain.

Around dawn on March 16, the main body of Greene's army reached the Speedwell Iron Works on Troublesome Creek. Still anticipating a British attack, the general at once set his men to work digging trenches. The officers were ordered to inspect their men's arms and equipment and to submit returns of their losses in the battle. The commissaries were directed to issue two days' rations and a gill of rum to each man.

While the night of March 15 was hard for the Americans, it was an absolute horror for the British forces encamped on the battlefield at Guilford Courthouse. The redcoats had eaten their last skimpy rations—four ounces of bread and an equal amount of lean beef per man—at 4 P.M. on March 14. Since then they had marched 12 miles, fought a series of heavy skirmishes, and won a

major battle. There were no immediate rewards for these extraordinary accomplishments, only more hardships. The commissaries had no food to issue the famished redcoats, nor was there
any shelter available from the cold and rain. Perhaps worst of all
was the emotional trauma of spending the night on a battlefield
littered with hundreds of dead and wounded British and American soldiers. Charles Stedman wrote a lengthy account of that
horrible night.

The night was remarkable for its darkness, accompanied with rain which
fell in torrents. Near fifty of the wounded, it is said, sinking under their
aggravated miseries, expired before the morning. The crys of the
wounded and dying, who remained on the field of action during the
night exceeded all description. Such a complicated scene of honor and
distress, it is hoped, for the sake of humanity, rarely occurs, even in a
military life.

The British devoted March 16 to the grisly tasks of burying
the dead and collecting the wounded. The injured redcoats were
evacuated to the New Garden Friends Meeting House and surrounding structures. Those Americans who had been too badly
hurt to retreat with their comrades were removed to the Guilford
Courthouse building. Details were sent out to scour the countryside for food.

As this work progressed, Cornwallis began to receive field
returns that allowed him to fully evaluate the previous day's
action. The British general obviously was pleased that his redcoats had driven off a numerically superior enemy army. The
fruits of this victory included four cannons, two ammunition
wagons, 1,300 stands of small arms, and a handful of rebel prisoners. Although he could not accurately ascertain the total American losses in killed and wounded, he believed they were "considerable."

These accomplishments were impressive, but, as Cornwallis
soon realized, they in no way compensated for the terrible injuries
inflicted upon his own army. According to Cornwallis's field
returns, 1,924 British and German troops of all ranks were
engaged in the Battle of Guilford Courthouse. Final reports indi-
cated that 93 men were killed, 413 were wounded, and 26 were

Col. Otho Holland Williams (1749-94). Mezzotint after painting by Charles Willson Peale.

listed as missing. This casualty total of 532 represented a staggering 27% of the British troops engaged.

Losses were particularly severe among the officer corps; 29 of the army's 100 officers were killed or wounded in the battle. Included among these were Lt. Col. James Stuart of the 2nd Battalion of Guards, killed on the third line; his superior, Brigadier General O'Hara, who suffered two dangerous wounds;

78   and Lieutenant Colonel Webster of the 33rd, who later died of his injuries. Deep in hostile territory, lacking provisions, and confronted by an increasingly aggressive enemy, the British army could ill afford the loss of many of its most experienced leaders.

By comparison, American losses were exceedingly light. Greene's army entered the Battle of Guilford Courthouse with approximately 4,400 men and his casualties were listed as 79 killed and 185 wounded. He also reported 1,046 men as missing, but in light of Cornwallis's remark that his army took few prisoners, it must be assumed that most of these missing were militiamen who escaped capture by scattering into the forest. Greene's adjutant, Col. Otho Williams, remarked that "many of those missing are expected to return, or to be found at their homes." Discounting the missing, American losses amounted to only 6% of the total force engaged.

As Cornwallis studied the lengthening casualty lists submitted by his officers, he realized that his army was in no condition to face the Americans again. Too many good soldiers were dead, too many wounded remained to be cared for, and those who could still shoulder a musket had gone too long without adequate food or clothing for Cornwallis to consider taking the offensive again. As Charles James Fox, a member of Parliament's antiwar minority, commented when news of the Battle of Guilford Courthouse reached London: "Another such victory would ruin the British army."

"We Fight, Get Beat, Rise, and Fight Again"

Cornwallis SPENT two and one-half days making preparations for his army to evacuate Guilford Courthouse. He planned to move his command first to Bell's Mill on the Deep River, "where the greatest number of our friends are said to reside." From Bell's Mill, Cornwallis intended to proceed southeast "by easy marches" toward Cross Creek—the head of navigation on the Cape Fear River—where he hoped to "procure the necessary supplies for further operations, and lodge our sick and wounded where proper attention can be paid them."

Before he began this withdrawal, Cornwallis directed his surgeons to separate the most dangerously wounded British and

Hessian troops from those who could travel. He also sent a message to Greene, informing him that he had issued orders to collect the American wounded, and asking that Greene "send immediately Surgeons to take care of them and a Supply of Necessaries and Provisions." Greene responded, thanking Cornwallis, and indicating that he had already dispatched surgeons and would send food and medical supplies.

British commissaries continued their efforts to find food, but met with only limited success. The shortage of provisions remained so acute that Cornwallis issued an address to his troops, assuring them that he was "thoroughly sensible of the distress they suffer for want of flower [sic] or meal," and explaining that they remained at Guilford Courthouse only to assure "the Safety of their Wounded Companions."

A few more tasks remained for the British to complete. A large number of rebel small arms had been picked up on the battlefield after the American withdrawal. Some of these weapons were distributed to the Tories in Hamilton's regiment and the remainder destroyed. Cornwallis also ordered that all prisoners of war, except those considered "dangerous," be paroled. On March 17, the earl sent off 17 wagons filled with the wounded "whose cases will admit of their being again with the army." The following afternoon, the British army marched away from Guilford Courthouse, leaving behind 64 of their most seriously wounded comrades, and a like number of injured Americans, in the care of the Quakers at New Garden.

Greene's army spent most of March 16 digging breastworks along Troublesome Creek. Their general was disappointed by the outcome of the battle, but was by no means downcast. In orders to his army, he characterized the defeat as "unfortunate, but by no means decisive." As reports of the poor condition of the British forces filtered in, he grew increasingly optimistic. By the morning of March 18, Greene's evaluation of the battle was markedly positive. He wrote Gov. Abner Nash of North Carolina:

The Enemy's loss is very great, much more than ours . . . [T]he enemy have gained no advantage, except the ground and field pieces. Their operating force is diminished in such a manner, that I am not without hope of turning their victory into defeat, if the Militia don't leave me.

Greene's concern about his militia forces was well founded. One of the general's staff wrote that within a few days after the battle, groups of militiamen began to make "one frivolous pretense and another to return home." Including men who ran away from the battlefield, perhaps 1,000 of the militia deserted. Greene was shortly forced to write to Gov. Thomas Jefferson of Virginia, asking him to call out 1,500 militia for three months service with his army.

When he received word of Cornwallis's departure from Guilford Courthouse, Greene decided to "follow them immediately, with the determination for another touch." Yet, it was March 20 before the American army actually broke camp to pursue the redcoats. This delay apparently was required so that the army's ammunition supply, seriously depleted in the fighting of March 15, could be replenished. Greene did, however, dispatch Lee's legion and Campbell's riflemen on March 19, "to hang upon the rear" of the British column. In his instructions to Lee, the commanding general wrote, "I mean to fight the enemy again, and wish you to have your Legion and riflemen ready for action on the shortest notice. In the mean time [if] you can attempt anything which promises an advantage, put it in execution."

When the Americans finally marched away from their Troublesome Creek lines, they retraced their steps back to Guilford Courthouse. The area's Quakers probably hoped that the Americans would take charge of the wounded that the British had left behind, but Greene had no intention of further delaying his pursuit or of encumbering his army with scores of wounded men. Like Cornwallis before him, Greene sent word to the gentle Quakers, asking them to care for these injured soldiers.

This imposition was but one of a series of hardships inflicted upon the Friends by the contending armies. For several weeks prior to March 15, the inhabitants of the New Garden community had been victimized by roving bands of foraging soldiers, and thieves disguised as soldiers, who stripped their homes of food, livestock, and valuables.

Their meeting house grounds had been profaned by fighting on the morning of the battle, and many Friends had since been displaced from their homes by the wounded. Now these hundreds of injured men were being abandoned in their midst. Nevertheless, the Quakers remained true to their principles and continued their ministrations to the wounded.

In addition to their losses of foodstores and other property, the Friends paid another high price for their selflessness: smallpox that had broken out among the British casualties took the lives of several members of the New Garden meeting.

On March 19, the British reached Bell's Mill, where they halted for two days to rest and collect supplies of meal and flour. In spite of British claims of victory at Guilford Courthouse, the loyalists, who were reported to be in the majority in this locale, could not be persuaded to take up arms against the rebels. The ragged appearance of the redcoats, their obvious hunger and fatigue, and the long ambulance train that followed them did little to inspire confidence in the king's arms. The threat of retaliation by Lee's cavalry also served to keep otherwise sympathetic Tories close to home.

Cornwallis commented sardonically that "Many of the Inhabitants rode into Camp, shook me by the hand, said they were glad to see us and to hear that we had beat Greene, and then rode home again . . . ." Disappointed, the British general led his troops down the Deep River toward Ramsey's Mill.

As the Americans marched away from Guilford Courthouse for the last time, they headed southeast, across South Buffalo Creek. They did not, however, move at top speed, for there still were "provisions to draw, cartridges to make, and several other matters to attend to . . . ." These logistical details were finally completed on March 23, and Greene resolved to attack the enemy without further delay.

The British army then was encamped at Ramsey's Mill, where Cornwallis had again halted to rest his wounded and to permit the commissaries to forage. The redcoats also hurriedly constructed a bridge across the Deep River to allow the army, its artillery, and its ambulance trains to cross easily to the south side of the channel.

On March 27, Greene's army approached to within 12 miles of the British camp and prepared to attack. The American general hoped to trap the redcoats against the banks of the Deep, and dispatched Lee to ford the river and seize their recently completed bridge from the south.

Cornwallis, however, discerned the enemy's intentions and, on March 28, pushed his troops rapidly across the river, burning the bridge behind them. The redcoats withdrew in such haste that they left unburied the bodies of several of their comrades who had succumbed to wounds. The British general drove his men on toward Cross Creek. When Lee's cavalrymen galloped up later that afternoon, they found only the British dead to greet them.

General Greene reached Ramsey's Mill the following day. There, along the banks of the Deep River, he decided to break off the chase. The armies had entered a sparsely populated region, aptly called the Pine Barrens, which extended almost to the coast. As Horatio Gates had discovered when he marched through this district on his way to Camden in 1780, there were not enough provisions in this desolate area to feed an army. Another factor in Greene's decision to call off the chase was his belief that he could not find replacements for the militiamen, who continued to leave his ranks in this "vile toryish country" of eastern North Carolina.

So, the American general elected to turn his column into South Carolina, where, with the assistance of local partisan bands, he hoped to eliminate a number of the redcoats' interior posts before Cornwallis could come to their assistance. By marching south, he also could afford to give North Carolina a respite from the months of campaigning that had disrupted the state since the autumn of 1780.

Greene need not have concerned himself about Cornwallis's intentions. When the British reached Cross Creek, Cornwallis discovered "to [his] great mortification, and contrary to all former accounts, that it was impossible to procure any considerable quantity of provisions, and that there was not four days forage within twenty miles." Likewise, he found that his hopes for shipping supplies up the Cape Fear River were "totally impractible."

The water route distance from Wilmington to Cross Creek was about 150 miles. The river was full of twists and turns, was seldom more than 100 yards wide inland, and its banks were often quite steep. American guerrillas could prey on British shipping along its entire course, firing down from the lofty riverbanks on the supply vessels. The earl concluded that his army must push on toward the friendly haven of Wilmington.

Wilmington had fallen on February 1, 1781, to Maj. James Craig and about 400 redcoats whom Cornwallis had ordered north from Charleston. Although Craig had been unable to ship supplies upriver to Cornwallis, he had captured a number of prominent rebel leaders and rallied considerable Tory support. Thus, Wilmington was the one spot in North Carolina where Cornwallis and his troops could enjoy a respite from their months of hardship.

The crippled British army limped into Wilmington on April 7, 1781. While his hungry men were fed and his surviving wounded cared for, the earl considered his remaining options. The day before, Greene's army had broken its camp at Ramsey's Mill and begun the march toward South Carolina. Conventional military reasoning would have required Cornwallis to lead his troops south either to fall on the rear of Greene's column or to join with Lord Rawdon's forces in South Carolina to repel the American invaders.

Cornwallis did neither. He believed it absolutely essential that his weary infantrymen have at least a brief rest before they undertook any more active campaigning. And, he questioned whether his army could reach South Carolina in time to play a decisive role in the coming battles. In any event, Cornwallis believed that Rawdon's forces were strong enough to defeat the rebels.

In truth, the "modern Hannibal's" thoughts were consumed more by plans for carrying the war into Virginia than with events in South Carolina. Cornwallis had become convinced that Virginia was the key to victory in the South.

Virginia was the largest, most populous, and richest of all the rebellious colonies. Throughout the campaign, Cornwallis had seen Greene's army use that state both as a sanctuary and as a source of supplies and reinforcements. In his opinion, as long as Virginia remained a hotbed of revolution, the British position in the Carolinas was untenable. Cornwallis now was convinced that the only way to successfully conclude the war was to concentrate British forces in Virginia, where "a successful battle may give us

America." With this in mind, he led his 1,435 redcoats out of Wilmington on August 25, 1781, on the first leg of a futile quest for the victory that had eluded him in North Carolina.

Cornwallis's decision to move into Virginia was unquestionably the greatest mistake of his long and distinguished military career. Although he would not admit it, his North Carolina campaign had been a complete failure. His superb troops had marched more than 1,000 miles through the interior of the state and had won one of the most fiercely contested battles of the war. Yet, they had failed to establish permanent British control over any part of the rebellious colony, and had also been unable to inspire more than token loyalist support for their cause. Most serious of all, Cornwallis failed to destroy Nathanael Greene's army, and he compounded this failure by allowing the rebels to march unopposed into South Carolina. By doing so, Cornwallis unwittingly sealed the fate of the British-held South.

In the coming months, Greene's troops fought four pitched battles and a number of smaller engagements in South Carolina. The American forces lost each of their major engagements in battles reminiscent of Guilford Courthouse. However, with remarkable persistence, Greene held his army together and refused to give up the offensive. As Greene put it, "We fight, get beat, rise, and fight again."

The presence of the Continentals, who cooperated with the Carolina partisans and militia, proved decisive, forcing the British to abandon one outpost after another. By July, 1781, the king's standard flew over only the cities of Savannah, Georgia, and Charleston, South Carolina, and its environs. Restricted to their seaboard bases, 6,000 redcoats heard the news that Lord Cornwallis had surrendered on October 18, 1781, to combined French and American forces at an obscure Virginia village called Yorktown.

The surrender at Yorktown did not bring the war to an immediate end. Cornwallis was not the commander-in-chief in America, and more important, there still were 20,000 redcoats in New York and in the southern garrisons who could have carried on the struggle. In fact, there was desultory fighting in Georgia as late as August, 1782, and the last redcoats did not sail out of Charleston harbor until the following December.

However, British reverses suffered in the South in 1781 made peace inevitable. Parliament and the English people would no longer support a war that took the lives of their young men, drained their national treasury, and, in return, brought only defeats, and victories that bore all the consequences of defeat.

This nineteenth-century engraving attempts to telescope action into a single episode.

Bibliography

Primary Sources

CONTEMPORARY HISTORIES

Clinton, Lt. Gen. Sir Henry. *Observations on Mr. Stedman's History of the American War*. London: 1794.

Gordon, William. *The History of the Rise, Progress, and Establishment of the Independence of the United States of America: Including an Account of the Late War, and of the Thirteen Colonies from Their Origin to That Period*. Vol. III. New York: 1801.

Mackenzie, Roderick. *"Strictures on Lt. Col. Tarleton's History" of the Campaigns of 1780 and 1781, in the Southern Provinces of North America*. London: 1787.

Marshall, John. *The Life of George Washington*. Vol. IV. Compiled under the direction of Bushrod Washington. Philadelphia: 1805.

Ramsay, David. *The History of the American Revolution*. Dublin: 1792.

Stedman, Charles. *The History of the Origin, Progress, and Termination of the American War*. Vol. II. Dublin: 1794.

Tarleton, Banastre. *A History of the Campaigns of 1780 and 1781 in the Southern Provinces of North America*. London and Dublin: 1787.

The Annual Register, or a View of the History, Politics and Literature for the Year 1781. London: 1782.

MEMOIRS, PAPERS, CORRESPONDENCE, PARTICIPANT ACCOUNTS

Boyd, Julian P., ed. *The Papers of Thomas Jefferson*. Vol. V. Princeton: 1952.

Clinton, Sir Henry. *American Rebellion: Sir Henry Clinton's Narrative of His Campaigns, 1775-1782, with an Appendix of Original Documents*. Edited by William B. Willicox. New Haven: 1954.

88   Lamb, Sgt. Robert. *Memoirs of His Own Life*. Dublin: 1811.

_____. *Original and Authentic Journal of Occurences During the Late American War, from Its Commencement to 1783*. Dublin: 1809.

Lee, Henry. *The Campaign of 1781 in the Carolinas: With Remarks Historical and Critical on Johnson's Life of Greene*. Reprint. Chicago: 1962.

_____. *Memoirs of the War in the Southern Department of the United States: A New Edition, with Revisions, and a Biography of the Author by Robert E. Lee*. New York: 1870.

Montross, Lynn. *Rag, Tag and Bobtail: The Story of the Continental Army, 1775-1783*. New York: 1952.

Seymour, William. "A Journal of the Southern Expedition, 1780-1783." *Historical and Biographical Papers of the Historical Society of Delaware*. Vol. II, Paper XV (1896).

Scheer, George F., and Rankin, Hugh F. *Rebels and Redcoats*. Cleveland: 1957.

Stevens, Benjamin Franklin, ed. *The Campaign in Virginia: An Exact Reprint of Six Rare Pamphlets on the Clinton-Cornwallis Controversy With Very Numerous Important Unpublished Manuscript Notes by Sir Henry Clinton*. 2 vols. London: 1888.

Tucker, St. George. "The Southern Campaign: 1781: From Guilford Court House to the Siege of York: Narrated in the Letters from Judge St. George Tucker to His Wife." *The Magazine of American History with Notes and Queries*, VII (1881), pp. 36-46.

REMINISCENCES, COMPILATIONS, AND ANECDOTES

Caldwell, Charles. *Memoirs of the Life and Campaigns of the Hon. Nathanael Greene*. Philadelphia: 1819.

Caruthers, Rev. Eli Washington. *Revolutionary Incidents: and Sketches of Character, Chiefly in the "Old North State."* Philadelphia: 1854.

_____. *A Sketch of the Life and Character of the Rev. David Caldwell*. Greensborough, N.C.: 1842.

Foote, William Henry. *Sketches of North Carolina, Historical and Biographical, Illustrative of the Principles of a Portion of Her Early Settlers*. 1846. Reprint. Raleigh, N.C.: 1965.

_____. *Sketches of Virginia, Historical and Biographical*. 2nd series, 2nd edition revised. Philadelphia: 1856.

Garden, Alexander. *Anecdotes of the Revolutionary War in America*. Charleston, S.C.: 1822.

Hoyt, William Henry, ed. *The Papers of Archibald D. Murphey*. Vol. II. [includes "General Joseph Graham's Narrative of the Revolutionary War in North Carolina in 1780 and 1781" (1821)]. Raleigh, N.C.: 1914.

Wheeler, John Hill. *Historical Sketches of North Carolina from 1584 to 1851*. Philadelphia: 1851.

Wyatt, Thomas. *Memoirs of the Generals, Commodores, and Other Commanders, Who Distinguished Themselves In The American Army and Navy During The Wars Of The Revolution and 1812, and Who Were Presented With Medals By Congress, For Their Gallant Services*. Philadelphia: 1848.

OFFICIAL RECORDS

The Colonial Records of North Carolina. Vol. VIII. Edited by William L. Saunders. Raleigh, N.C.: 1890.

Newsome, A. R., ed. "A British Orderly Book, 1780-1781." *North Carolina Historical Review*, IX, 1932.

The State Records of North Carolina. Vols. 16-25. Edited by Walter Clark *et al*. Goldsboro, N.C.: 1899-1907.

Secondary Sources

THE REVOLUTIONARY WAR

Alden, John Richard. *The American Revolution: 1775-1783*. New York: 1954.

Boatner, Mark M. *Encyclopedia of the American Revolution*. Vol. III. New York: 1966.

Commager, Henry Steele, and Morris, Richard B. *Spirit of Seventy-Six: The Story of the American Revolution as Told by Participants*. 1958. Reprint. New York: 1967.

Hatch, Charles E. *The Battle of Guilford Courthouse*. Washington, D.C.: 1971.

Newlin, Algie I. *The Battle of New Garden*. Greensboro, N.C.: 1977.

Rankin, Hugh F. *The American Revolution*. New York: 1964.

_____. *The North Carolina Continentals*. Chapel Hill, N.C.: 1971.

_____. *North Carolina in the American Revolution*. Raleigh, N.C.: 1959.

Schenck, David. *North Carolina, 1780-1781: Being a History of the Invasion of the Carolinas*. Raleigh, N.C.: 1889.

90   BIOGRAPHY

Graham, James. *The Life of General Daniel Morgan of the Virginia Line of the Army of the United States with Portions of His Correspondence Compiled from Authentic Sources.* New York: 1856.

Greene, George Washington. *The Life of Nathanael Greene, Major General in the Army of the Revolution.* Vol. III. New York: 1871.

Heitman, Francis B. *Historical Register of Officers of the Continental Army During the War of the Revolution.* Boston: 1967.

North Carolina Biographical Sketches of the Soldiers and Patriots in the Battle of Guilford Courthouse, March 15, 1781. Greensboro, N.C.: issued serially 1958-1963.

Thayer, Theodore George. *Nathanael Greene: Strategist of the American Revolution.* New York: 1960.

Wickwire, Franklin, and Wickwire, Mary. *Cornwallis: The American Adventure.* Boston: 1970.